RESEARCH on
MAIN STREET

RESEARCH on MAIN STREET

Using the Web to Find
Local Business and Market Information

Marcy Phelps

CyberAge Books
Medford, New Jersey

First Printing, 2011

Research on Main Street: Using the Web to Find Local Business and Market Information

Library of Congress Cataloging-in-Publication Data

Phelps, Marcy, 1950-
    Research on Main Street : using the web to find local business and market information / Marcy Phelps
        p. cm.
    Includes index.
    ISBN 978-0-910965-88-0
    1. Business information services--Computer network resources. 2. Small business--Computer networks. 3. Web sites. I. Title.
    HF54.56.P47 2011
    025.06'3386--dc22

                                                                        2010052245

Printed and bound in the United States of America

President and CEO: Thomas H. Hogan, Sr.
Editor-in-Chief and Publisher: John B. Bryans
Managing Editor: Amy M. Reeve
VP Graphics and Production: M. Heide Dengler
Book Designer: Kara Mia Jalkowski
Cover Designer: Lisa Conroy

www.infotoday.com

To my husband, Art, for your unfailing love,
support, and sense of humor.
Thank you for seeing things in me
that I don't see in myself.

Contents

Acknowledgments

I would like to thank the many people who helped me through the entire process of writing *Research on Main Street*. This was truly a group effort, and I could not have completed the book without any of you.

Many, many thanks go to Mary Ellen Bates. Your support and coaching helped make this book a reality and not just a dream—and your editing skills made it so much better. Thanks to Kim Dority who, with Mary Ellen, is part of our SSW group. You've been a wonderful mentor through the years and have helped me set and reach some pretty big goals.

Thanks to Christine Hamilton-Pennell for letting me pick your brain about a tough topic: local economics. I also want to thank the members of the Association of Independent Information Professionals (www.aiip.org) for answering all the locally focused questions I've been asking through our email discussion list, AIIP-L. It's an honor to be part of a profession with so many brilliant and generous people.

Thanks definitely go to John Bryans, my publisher at Information Today, Inc., for this opportunity—and for your incredible patience.

Special thanks go to my dear husband, Art. I'm not sure how you've put up with me through this.

Finally, I want to thank the many generous individuals who contributed "Tips From the Pros" to the book, including Robert Berkman, Barbara Fullerton, Peggy Garvin, Christine Hamilton-Pennell, Amelia Kassel, Margaret King, Kathy Mills, Monnie Nilsson, Risa Sacks, and Cynthia Shamel. You've helped make this book richer.

About the Website

ResearchOnMainStreet.com

Web links quickly get stale, so be sure to visit the companion website for this book, ResearchonMainStreet.com. This site includes a list of all the resources mentioned in the book, and links will be updated on a regular basis. I'll also add more sources as I find them. If you have some favorite sites for local business research, send them to me at mphelps@phelpsresearch.com, and I'll post them with your name.

Enjoy this book and the website as you find the quickest route to high-quality local business information.

Disclaimer

Neither the publisher nor the author make any claim as to the results that may be obtained through the use of this webpage or of any of the internet resources it references or links to. Neither publisher nor author will be held liable for any results, or lack thereof, obtained by the use of this page or any of its links; for any third-party charges; or for any hardware, software, or other problems that may occur as the result of using it. This webpage is subject to change or discontinuation without notice at the discretion of the publisher and author.

Foreword

Timing is everything. Marcy sent me a draft of this book to review at the same time that my best client called me. The client, who always asks for broad consumer trends, urgently needed demographics on several "Metropolitan Divisions"—whatever those were! I vaguely knew that I'd find lots of information at the Census Bureau—I mean, that's what it's there for, right? I quickly found out that you can easily get buried in stats and still not find the ones you need.

Realizing that I could spend several hours noodling around Census.gov, I opened up the file Marcy sent me for Chapter 4, Local Demographics. Sure enough, I found a road map there to get me exactly what I was looking for. The time I saved by relying on Marcy's expertise rather than suffering through my own learning curve was significant, particularly since I bill my clients for my time.

What surprised me the most in reading through the rest of the chapters in *Research on Main Street* was realizing that a lot of business and market research projects have a local component. Now that I know more about local searching, I am finding that there are a lot of research questions that would benefit from a local perspective.

Say you need to scope out your organization's largest competitors. National Widgets Inc., the Google of the widget industry, is headquartered in Seattle, Washington. Through your diligent research, you discover that it is planning on moving its entire research and development (R&D) staff to a suburb of Dallas, Texas. You know that it is counting on most of its professional staff making the move to Dallas, and you recognize that as an opportunity. You pull together some statistics on local schools, community diversity, tax rates, cultural opportunities, and the general employment picture (knowing that the spouses of the relocated staff may need to find jobs there, too). You can now use a headhunter to contact the key members of the R&D staff, show them the comparison of the two geographic regions, and see whether you can entice them into switching jobs instead of states. What originally looked like research for a generic, national-level industry profile in the widget industry turned into a project requiring familiarity with a variety of sources for detailed, city-level information.

Here's a related (and sadly) real-life example. In 2010, I followed the news as the BP oil disaster in the Gulf of Mexico unfolded. BP itself went hyperlocal by streaming the video from remotely operated cameras a mile deep on the ocean floor. But I also wanted to see what happened to that gushing oil when it hit land. Most of the coverage of the oil spill was from a national perspective, so I headed straight over to the local news sources to get a ground-level perspective on how effective the cleanup was, the impact on the local economy, the needs of local volunteers and charities, and so on. Nothing can compete with local coverage when the news is itself a local event.

One other way I tracked the oil spill was through Twitter. BP has a Twitter feed for disseminating news as do most of the local and national news sources. As one approach after another was attempted to stop the spill, I got almost real-time updates. What I find telling is that I have come to expect this level of coverage. I expect to have real-time video streaming to me from the ocean floor.

In fact, one of the most interesting aspects of the social or collaborative web is the increased demand for and interest in personalized, localized content and resources. As Marcy points out in Chapter 2, Packing the Essentials, social media exist to facilitate human interaction, and humans tend to be local creatures who often talk about their local area. That drives the development of new tools to mine all that user-created local content. As business researchers, we now have the opportunity to gather more and much deeper local-level information than we could by using only the static web. The business research we provide offers more facets and perspectives when we tap into all that local content. It also means that we will be called on by our organizations to know more about local-level trends as people realize that 1) learning about and interacting with the business environment at the local level is a good business decision and 2) local-level information isn't something you can just Google—the information is on the web, but it isn't easy to find.

That's why *Research on Main Street* is such a tremendous resource. Throughout the book, Marcy offers short case studies that I found really helpful in understanding when I could use these resources in *my* day-to-day work. This book covers an area of business research that simply hasn't been addressed before, and it fills an important gap in any researcher's toolkit.

—Mary Ellen Bates,
BatesInfo.com

Introduction

Several years ago, I spoke with a conference program planner about my upcoming presentation for her organization. I had sent her several topics related to business research, on which I frequently speak and write, and the purpose of our call was to narrow down the list of possibilities. After a few minutes of discussion, she said, "Marcy, these are great topics, but could you possibly talk about local market research?" I did, and it became one of my most requested speaking topics.

As with any new presentation, I invested a lot of time in researching this topic and talking about it with other librarians and information professionals. I looked back on my own experience with client projects that involved finding and analyzing information about small local areas, and I spoke with business professionals across a range of industries.

Through my research, I found that even in our global economy, businesses are still hungry for targeted, localized information about customers, companies, and trends. It doesn't matter whether you're in a Fortune 500 company or a one-person operation. If you're entering a new market, tracking competitors, identifying possible strategic partners, getting to know your buyers, or raising funds, you're probably asking questions about specific—and sometimes very small—geographic areas. And as with any type of research, you're looking for answers on the web.

Entrepreneurs deciding on a location for their new businesses depend on neighborhood-level demographics. Large organizations seeking partners to help them connect with customers in certain geographic markets want information about local companies, events, or issues. Nonprofits need community-level information to help them learn about potential donors and monitor awareness levels. In an age of limited budgets and high accountability, people are discovering that each county, city, town, and neighborhood is unique and that national- or state-level information won't always tell them what they need to know.

What I also found through my research for the presentation on local market research and through my work with clients is that adding the element of geography to any search topic—especially for counties, cities, census blocks, or any other substate area—will make any project a lot more challenging. For several reasons, even the most experienced business researchers expressed frustration with this topic.

First, the people I talked and worked with said they need high-quality information since they use it for making important business decisions. Too often, inserting a local aspect into a search means a search results page full of city guides, restaurant reviews, and meet-ups. While these can yield some useful information, most searchers needed more business-oriented, reliable sources—and they weren't finding them.

Second, Google and other general-purpose search engines don't do a good job of localizing search results. Few web resources go to the local level, and those that do can be expensive. Many sources frequently offer information that's out-of-date, not very in-depth, or lacking in local feel. It can be quite time-consuming to drill down to information about just one particular place or to compare information about several small locations.

Finally, many people I spoke with said that even if they could find local demographics and other numbers, something was still missing. Without any insider knowledge of the target group and location, they risked making mistakes in their critical business decisions. They wanted to check statistics, gather some opinions, and get the "real story."

For all these reasons, finding business information on the local level became a popular speaking topic for me and is why I wrote

Research on Main Street. If you are involved in starting, running, or building a business in any way, at some point you are going to need to find local-level information to help you fill in the gaps or make decisions. But it shouldn't be such a difficult task. Although they're sometimes hard to find, good local sources exist, and new ones are introduced almost daily. You just have to know where to look, and you need a few tips to make the process go quickly and smoothly.

About This Book

Research on Main Street is a guide to using free and low-cost options on the web to find business and market information about local places. It also shows how to use local sources for more in-depth research into people, companies, and national issues that impact certain parts of the country.

This book covers how to approach this type of research, key resources, and practical solutions to specific questions. My goal is to help you find better local-level information in less time—even if you don't have a big budget.

The book is organized as follows: Chapters 1 through 3 provide a framework for researching local information. They introduce you to local business research, including what makes it unique, how to approach it, and what types of resources will give you the best results. Chapter 3 is devoted to making sure you're using quality sources, avoiding online scams and misinformation, and respecting copyright, among other topics.

Chapters 4 through 8 examine various types of local information, with chapters on local demographics, economics, companies, people, and issues. Each chapter includes strategy tips and resources, and—to show you how it's all put into action—a section of examples illustrating when each type of information might be needed and how it can be found.

The last chapter of this book and the two appendixes offer several advanced tools and resources that streamline the process of local business research even further. Chapter 9 covers using fee-based information sources to find local information. Appendix A lists all the resources mentioned in this book, arranged by chapter, with a brief description of each, providing useful topic-based guides to key local sources. Appendix B includes short guides with everyday business and market research questions and sites for finding the answers.

As a bonus, all chapters include valuable Tips From the Pros. These short sections spotlight expert researchers, who share their advice for finding local business and market information.

While the book as a whole will give you a comprehensive overview of the topic, each chapter can be used as a focused and practical stand-alone component. This way, *Research on Main Street* can be read straight through or a chapter at a time. I recommend, however, that you at least scan Chapter 1, Planning the Trip, before starting the others. It lays the foundation and explains the rules of the road, including some of the challenges involved with local research and suggestions for working around them.

What You Won't Find in This Book

To make this book as practical as possible, I have focused on U.S. information and sources. While you won't find specific resources for other countries here, the principles and general framework presented can be applied globally. I encourage you to see how the strategies discussed in *Research on Main Street* can be used for other regions.

You also won't find coverage of public records research. Many local research projects involve searching publicly available government documents. Public records research, however, requires a very specialized set of tools and skills and is best left to the experts.

Often, the quickest route to local information is not through the web but through "offline" methods such as focus groups or phone conversations with experts. *Research on Main Street* focuses on web-based research and shows you how to use the web to identify people to contact when what you're looking for isn't online or when you need to verify what you have found. It also provides some tips for preparing for your conversations and getting people to answer your questions.

Local is becoming synonymous with *mobile*. I've chosen not to include sources that are available only through mobile search since, at this time, 1) business-grade content and applications are few and far between and 2) most business researchers don't do professional research on their mobile phones.

Finally, this book doesn't attempt to cover all local-related resources, and it would be impossible to try. Consider *Research on Main Street* as your guide, brimming with useful strategies and sources for finding quality local-level business information on the web.

CHAPTER ONE

Planning The Trip: How To Approach Local Business Research

Before going local—before you use the web to find business and market information—you have to prepare for the ride. Finding the kind of authoritative local information you need when you're making important decisions can be time-consuming, and it's not always cheap.

Local business information is very specialized, and it's costly to create. You'll find fewer online resources covering small geographic areas than those containing global, national, or even state-level information. Those that do provide detailed, local-level information will often charge a fee. Governments, associations, and other organizations within smaller geographic locations sometimes don't have the staff or budget needed to compile or maintain sources.

You'll make the best use of your local research time and dollars if you have a strategy—one that will direct you to the best sources and help you quickly drill to the local level. As with any good plan, your strategy for finding local business sources and information should include some flexibility, creativity, and a selection of alternative routes, just in case you don't come across exactly what you need. When you're researching a local area or using local sources for more in-depth coverage of a topic, where do you start?

Take a Geography Lesson

It sounds basic, but before you get started, make sure you learn a little about your targeted location. Are you researching Lakewood, Colorado, or Lakewood, California? In which county or metropolitan area is this neighborhood found? When working on a geography-based project, I like to run a search in Google Maps (maps.google.com) to view the boundaries and nearby places. A county or city website could also be a good starting point for learning about a location and might quickly lead you to some key resources.

In addition to learning about locations, your search for local information will be easier if you become familiar with some basic geographic concepts, including terminology and the various ways geographic areas can be broken down. Chapter 4, Local Demographics, covers some definitions and a brief discussion of geography types. *Demographics: A Guide to Methods and Data Sources for Media, Business, and Government,* by Steve Murdock, Chris Kelley, Jeffrey Jordan, Beverly Pecotte, and Alvin Luedke (Paradigm Publishers, 2006), includes a nice description of common ways that geography can be delineated.

Small Locations Don't Live in Isolation

More often than not, local business and market research shouldn't be limited to a particular geographic location. What happens in one location influences, and is influenced by, what's going on elsewhere.

Local economies, for example, are often directly affected by state and national economic conditions. That's why it's a good idea to look at information about a geographic area in the following contexts:

- How it relates to *larger* geographic areas: Find out if the information about a location is consistent with what's happening on a national or state level. For example, many sources for local statistics include tables with comparisons to larger areas.

- How it relates to *nearby* geographic areas: Consider how information about one place compares with what is known about other cities, towns, or neighborhoods in the region. Can you find and easily compare, for example, the demographics of the cities and towns in a particular county?

- How it relates to *similar* geographic areas in other regions: Compare the findings for one location with others that are similar in size, demographics, climate, or other factors. As an example, you might want to see how one city's job-growth numbers look when compared with those of similar-sized cities in other parts of the country.

Take Time for a Reality Check

As I've said earlier in this chapter and in this book's introduction, when it comes to local business and market information, you're not always going to find exactly what you want. With all research, it's essential to manage your expectations from the very beginning, and this step is perhaps even more important when searching for local information.

Start by listing and evaluating your key questions:

- Prioritize the list so you can determine what information is essential and what's just "nice to know." More information is not necessarily better, and having too much will get in the way of what's really important.

- Check to see that the questions on your list aren't too specific. It's often easier to keep your questions more general and not impose too many limits on your search. For example, instead of searching for several specific economic indicators, try pulling in any of the indicators that you find that could help you piece together a picture of your location.

- Stop at regular intervals throughout the research process to review your priorities and revise your tactics. You might discover that in light of what you've found, a different approach might be more fruitful. You might also decide that the time is right to end your search.

Managing Your Clients' Expectations

Cynthia Shamel, Shamel Information Services

Managing expectations is an important part of managing clients and projects. Clear, open, and ongoing communication will lead to a mutual understanding about the scope, the deliverable, the costs, and the timeline. Whenever possible, negotiate all these parameters before you begin work. They are interdependent, and one will affect the other. Monitor the variables as you go along. Should anything change, notify your client immediately and renegotiate. It doesn't matter what triggers the change; it could be the client expanding the scope, the costs running higher than anticipated, or more time being required to analyze results. Whatever triggers the change, it is your responsibility to keep the four variables of scope, deliverable, costs, and timeline in balance. Be prepared to give and take, and then communicate the options to your client.

For example, a client recently asked for a complex research project with a short time frame and a specific format for delivering results. We agreed on a project strategy, and the client approved the anticipated costs. As work progressed, the client requested changes to the final report that significantly increased the time required to complete the project. We discussed alternatives. The scope, the due date, and the desired deliverable were nonnegotiable. The only variable to adjust was cost. Only by increasing the project budget could we meet the client's changed expectations. When we explained this to her, she agreed to the increase. Client expectations had been managed clearly and openly so that everyone was satisfied.

Effective client relations rely on trust. It is your responsibility to facilitate the communication necessary to develop a mutual understanding that will lead to an on-time, on-budget, on-target project outcome. Exceed expectations, and you can build the trust you need to encourage repeat business and to generate referrals.

Be Flexible

When it comes to local business research, you need to consider that the information you're looking for may never have been gathered or posted on a website. Even if it exists, what if it becomes too costly for you to find? You will have better results if you're flexible about the questions you're asking.

With local research, it's especially important to consider what's "good enough" for your project or what else would answer your ultimate questions. The following are the kinds of questions you could be asking yourself or your clients in order to add some flexibility to your local research projects:

- If data from the decennial census is not fresh enough, will the latest estimates from the American Community Survey suffice?

- Could 3-year estimates make a good substitute if projections turn out to be too costly?

- Would county-level data be good enough if city-level data isn't available?

Taking the time to answer these types of questions before you even start your search actually saves time in the long run. By not limiting yourself to just a specific set of hard-to-find data, you'll expand your options and possibly uncover something else that might be useful. Finally, you'll avoid spending time and money retrieving information that your client doesn't want.

Throw In a Little Creativity

When it comes to local business and market information, sometimes what you need won't be found in the most logical place. It often takes some creativity to gather the best information in the shortest amount of time. Here are some ways you can be more creative in your local searching:

- Think broadly about geography rather than focusing on a particular location. State websites, for example, often contain city-level data that's more detailed than what is found on a city's own website.

- As Mary Ellen Bates often says in her workshops and writings, it helps to "look sideways." Avoid staying too focused on just a precise set of sources or questions. While you're looking for and using local sources, keep an open mind and always consider other possibilities.

- Try using sources in creative ways. As an example, ThomasNet (www.thomasnet.com) is a free database of manufacturers, distributors, and service providers. It's marketed as something that, according to its website, "helps industrial businesses grow" and bring buyers to their own websites. For local researchers, though, it's also a great resource for counting and identifying companies by industry and location.

- Know when to stop or revise your search. If you're not finding the answers to your questions, think about taking another course of action. Would putting any more time into your current approach really uncover those golden nuggets of information, or will you just find more of the same?

Use the Web to Find Sources Rather Than Just Answers

Even with the most sophisticated search tools, business-quality local information is often elusive. Perhaps there's not much demand, so no one takes the time to gather or share the information. Sometimes, there's so much demand that the only online information you can find is contained in a high-priced packaged report. And at other times, it just isn't there. Yes, even in the age of Google and advanced information technology, not everything is online.

You'll increase the likelihood of eventually finding what you need if, rather than looking just for answers, you also look for sources that can lead you to your answers. While you're following the trail, stop to look around for a website, an organization, or a person that could be a source or could lead you to some likely sources. The following sections include tips for using the web to search for sources rather than just answers.

Look for Links and References to Sources

Lists of someone else's sources of the information they're providing, or links to their favorite websites, are those "bread crumbs" found along the research trail that can lead you to your answer. They'll sometimes take you from a so-so resource to one that's right on target. Whenever you're scanning an association website, look for lists of links to relevant online resources. Make note of the people writing articles in your topic area, and look at what resources they turn to for local information. This will increase both the quantity and the quality of sources you use for your own research.

Just remember that in a hyperlinked world, it's easy to become distracted. You don't want to spend too long on any one site, and you definitely don't want to wander aimlessly from site to site. It's always important to have a plan for your research, stay focused, and keep an eye on the time you're spending online.

Identify People You Can Ask

Look for the experts since they may know the answers to your questions. Experts will often share unpublished research or articles. They can add local knowledge to any topic, and they can confirm what you've found on the web. Many are flattered and are quite generous when someone politely asks about their area of expertise. Here are some techniques for using the web to identify people to ask for help:

- Scan websites, databases, and other sources for people who have special knowledge of your topic or location. Find out who are considered the "local experts." For example, who is writing in local publications or speaking to local groups about your topic?

- Ask yourself who cares about this topic enough to study it, gather information about it, or spend some time talking about it. Look for local journalists, university professors, librarians, and people affiliated with local governments and associations.

- Check company websites for local management and staff. Even if these people don't have the answers you need, perhaps they are in a position to know who does.

Chapter 7, Looking for Locals, includes additional tips for using the web to identify local experts.

Prepare for the Interview

Once you've identified people to ask, use the web to prepare for your conversations with them. As any professional telephone researcher will tell you, the better you prepare for your initial call or email, the better your results. Unlike online research, if you make a mistake on your first interview, you don't get another chance to ask your question. If the experts don't have to explain the basics to you, they can spend more time going into specifics. These are some ways to prepare for conversations with the experts:

- Familiarize yourself with the vocabulary and the issues involved in their line of work. You will sound more informed, and you will be more likely to

quickly take in the information that the expert is
trying to convey.

- List your questions ahead of time, and be clear about
  your intent. Do you need specific information to fill
  in a gap in your knowledge? Are you trying to
  resolve an issue of conflicting information, or are
  you merely trying to get an expert opinion?

- Make sure you've been thorough in your web
  searching so that you don't waste your time and that
  of your contact by asking for information that can be
  found easily through online sources.

- Pick up the phone rather than sending an email. It's
  unlikely that someone will take the time to write out
  an answer, particularly when the delete key is so
  much more convenient.

Chapter 7, Looking for Locals, goes into more depth about turning to the experts and preparing for your interviews, and it includes
tips for getting people to talk.

Verify What You Find

It's always a good idea to take a cautious approach to using the web
for business- and market-related information. When you're looking
for information about a particular topic *and* a specific location, you've
added yet another level of uncertainty on top of your usual skepticism.
Pay special attention to the details of your sources and the information they contain to make sure that you're basing important business
decisions on sound information. For example, you might

- Compare statistics from different sources and look
  for any inconsistencies.

- Confirm that you have the most up-to-date information available.

- Make sure to separate fact from opinion.

You can use other online materials to verify the information, but sometimes it's quicker and simpler to call someone and ask. It also helps if you maintain a list of authoritative sources—known for their high-quality information—that you can turn to when you need to do local-level research. Appendix A, Resource Roadmap, is a good starting point and includes all the resources mentioned in this book, organized by chapter.

Know When It's Time to Pay

Sometimes, even for expert researchers, what's needed can't be found in free resources. Information, in spite of what people often think, is not always free. It takes time and expense to collect data, organize it, add analysis, package and distribute it, and do whatever else needs to be done to make the information accurate and useful. Free information is often provided through sponsorships or donations. Other times, it might be part of an organization's mission, or it's required by law. Otherwise, costs need to be recovered.

If you limit yourself to only what's available for free, you might be missing out on valuable information that can't be found elsewhere. You also risk spending more time looking for a free source than you would have spent by going to one that's fee-based. Chapter 9, Paying at the Pump, discusses specific fee-based sources that won't break your budget and describes what local information they contain and when to consider using them.

More Strategic Tips for Finding Local Business and Market Information

⇨ Before getting started, ask yourself or your client what's needed and how it will be used. Do you really need "everything there is to know" about a location, or will a few demographics or economic indicators meet your needs?

⇨ Use a variety of sources, and become familiar with both free and fee-based resources before you need them. This knowledge will come in handy when you're suddenly faced with a project or if you're pressed for time.

⇨ Always have a Plan B, just in case you can't find the answers to your questions. Look for what else you could use in their place. For example, will information about the number of jobs in a particular region substitute for payroll amounts?

⇨ Stop at regular intervals and take stock of your progress. Based on the amount of time or money spent, what do you have to show for it? Should you continue your web search, take some time to contact a few experts, or just end your research?

Packing the Essentials: Key Resources for Local Business Research

While the number of websites with a local focus grows almost daily, when you're looking for local-level strategic business information, you need resources that

1. Cover your topic

2. Provide the right local coverage

3. Include accurate, authoritative information

Unfortunately, finding sources that meet all three requirements can be difficult and time-consuming. So where do you turn for local business research?

This chapter includes an overview of the kinds of resources that can be used to find local-level business and market information, plus a brief description of each. It also discusses their pros and cons, how to locate them, and what you'll find in these resources.

So Many Choices

Before getting into specific resources, here are some of the various types of information sources that you can expect to encounter:

- Some resources provide just local information, while others mix local and nonlocal. *Local-only* coverage can be spotty and often lacks uniformity, but not all national or global resources go to the local level.

- There's local, and then there's *hyperlocal.* Hyperlocal sources focus on small geographic areas, usually at the community level. More than just classifieds or movie listings, hyperlocal sources contain consumer opinion, provide insights into local issues, and point you to local experts.

- While most business and market information will be in text or tables, you'll find valuable information in a *variety of formats.* Images, video, or audio connected to a particular geographic area may add information that can't be found through the printed word.

- The growth of blogs, online communities, mashups, and other *social media*—especially on the local level—has greatly increased the number of sources available to the local researcher. More and more researchers are adding social media resources to their searches.

- As with any type of research, at some point in your search for local business information, you need to make the choice between using *free* or *fee-based sources.* The decision depends on several factors, including budget and time frame. Remember, though, that fee-based sources often save search time and provide information not found in free sources.

Chapter 9, Paying at the Pump, covers some low-cost options for premium web content. Also, be sure to check your own local public library to see what fee-based sources it offers to residents through its websites and to learn the rules for using them.

So what are some specific resources for finding local business and market information? While the following list is by no means complete, it includes the most likely places to go for high-quality local information.

People Resources

Why would a book about finding information on the web list people at the top of the list of key resources? Talking with people is often the quickest route to the answers you need. Perhaps no one has had a chance to post the most recent statistics to the web. Sometimes, you'll find an expert who is still in the process of reporting research findings but who is willing to send you a preview of the results. Then there's the information you won't find in any data table, news headline, or other source. As competitive-intelligence researcher Ben Gilad puts it, "Only human sources can provide commentary, opinion, feelings, intuition, emotions, and commitment."[1]

Several issues need to be considered when including people resources in your local business research:

- Unlike web searching, human sources can't be queried anonymously. Before picking up the phone to call someone, consider these confidentiality issues: Will making the call, or will any of the questions you ask, give away competitive information? Determine whether you want to call attention to what you're doing.

- What information can you share with the person you are contacting? Decide ahead of time whether you can provide any details about your research or a summary of your findings.

- Can you get this information through legal and ethical means? Keep in mind that ethical researchers don't lie or misrepresent themselves to others, ever.

People in the following professions make good targets for your research because they generally keep an eye on the community and will often have subject expertise as well:

- Journalists

- Government workers

- Librarians

- University professors

- Association members or leaders

- Economists

- Economic development executives

Use web resources to find the right people to ask, and always scan for contact information and organizational charts. If the people you talk to don't have the answers to your questions, ask if they know who does. Chapter 7, Looking for Locals, explores the topic of finding experts and getting the most from your conversations.

Government Resources

Governments of all types and sizes collect local business and market information, and more and more are sharing it on the web. Where you head for local-level information can depend a lot on 1) what information you need and 2) what you will do with it. Going straight to a local government entity for information about businesses and the economy within its jurisdiction may be the most direct route to what you need. However, if you're researching multiple locations, you might consider starting with national sources because information from the federal government may contain local information from all the cities, counties, or other geographic entities.

Federal Government Resources

The federal government collects and analyzes massive amounts of data, much of it about local areas. Population and business statistics, economic indicators, regional profiles, and mapped data are made available for free through a variety of publications and databases. Many federal sources uniformly cover local areas, and several include useful tools for comparing multiple locations.

Selecting the key federal resources that match your needs can be confusing. In recent years, the U.S. government has created several web directories and other tools to make it easier to mine its data, but it's still difficult to find the sources that drill down to the local level unless you know exactly where you're going. When working with U.S. government resources, you'll also discover that many products use the same core data, but they present the information through of a variety of websites.

I've found that the most useful local-level business information comes from three U.S. government agencies: the Census Bureau, the Bureau of Economic Analysis, and the Bureau of Labor Statistics. These and other resources from the federal government are discussed in more detail in Chapters 4 through 8 of this book, including how you can use them to find information related to local demographics, economies, companies, people, and issues.

Census Bureau

The U.S. Census Bureau (www.census.gov) offers a vast collection of information about people, households, businesses, and industries, and several of its products break down the data into small local areas. In the Geography section of the site, you can become familiar with all the geographic units found in Census Bureau products, such as blocks, tracts, or county subdivisions. A full listing of programs and services from this agency can be found through its Publications link.

When most people think of the Census Bureau, the first thing that comes to mind is the decennial census, a population and housing survey that occurs in years that end in a zero. However, several of this agency's products contain between-census information that is more current.

The Census Bureau's key local resources are especially hard to find, mostly because they're scattered across a variety of websites. For example, you can get to county business patterns data at the Census Bureau's website, as well as through the American FactFinder and CenStats sites. Adding to the confusion, there's no centralized geographic guide to the Census Bureau's resources. In my experience, the following are some of the best sites for substate-level information from the Census Bureau.

American FactFinder: The principle access point for the results from the decennial census, the American FactFinder website (factfinder.census.gov) includes results from a number of other surveys as well. Many of these surveys offer local-level data that can easily be turned into custom data sets, maps, and quick tables:

- American Community Survey: An annual survey of 3 million households, the American Community Survey collects such information as age, race, income, commute time to work, home value, and veteran status. You can easily create geographic comparison tables for congressional districts, counties, school districts, and other local areas.

- Population Estimates: Based on decennial census data, estimates are released throughout the year in increasing geographic detail. Again, you can create tables that make it easy to compare geographic areas.

- Economic Census: Conducted every 5 years, this product offers profiles of local economies. Geographic area definitions, maps, and boundary changes can be found under the User Guide tab.

- County Business Patterns (CBP): Here you will find annual data, including the number of establishments, first quarter and annual payroll, and employment. Through the American FactFinder website, you can get CBP data for counties and metropolitan/ micropolitan statistical areas from 2004 forward in handy maps and quick tables. For ZIP code levels and pre-2004 CBP numbers, you'll need to go through the CenStats website, discussed next.

Search American FactFinder by geography by clicking the Search link at the top of the main page. Under the Geography tab, enter your location and select the year and census program.

CenStats Databases: Through CenStats (censtats.census.gov), the Census Bureau provides the following sources for local business information, all of which you can easily get to from the CenStats main page:

- CBP: CenStats' version of CBP includes employment and earnings by U.S. county, metropolitan statistical area, and ZIP code from 1998 forward.

- Building Permits: This database covers construction statistics (by permit-issuing place and by county) on new privately owned residential housing units authorized by building permits.

- USA Counties: With more than 6,000 data items on the county level, USA Counties is updated every 2 years.

Census Bureau Website: The Census Bureau's main website (www.census.gov) provides yet another gateway to its products. The main directory can lead you to resources covering people and households, business and industry, and other topics. You'll find useful census information about local areas through these sites:

- Small Area Income and Poverty Estimates (SAIPE; www.census.gov/did/www/saipe): The SAIPE program offers annual estimates of income and poverty indicators for all states, counties, and school districts.

- State and Metropolitan Area Data Book (www. census.gov/compendia/smadb): This includes more than 1,500 data items from a variety of sources for the U.S. and individual states, counties, and metropolitan and micropolitan areas.

- County and City Data Book (www.census.gov/statab/ www/ccdb.html): Look here for data on people and businesses for all U.S. states, counties, and cities with populations of 25,000 or more, with additional data for cities and towns with populations of 100,000 or more. You'll also find a complete set of state maps showing all counties, cities, and towns with populations of 25,000 or more, and metropolitan areas.

- State and County QuickFacts (quickfacts.census.gov/ qfd): A place for quick access to statistics about people, business, and geography, this site includes states, counties, cities, and towns with more than 25,000 people.

- Nonemployer Statistics (www.census.gov/econ/
  nonemployer): This annual data series covers
  businesses without paid employees, which are
  excluded from most sources of business statistics. In
  addition to national-level information, it provides
  data at the state, county, and metropolitan/
  micropolitan statistical area levels.

More about using Census Bureau resources for local business and market research can be found in Chapter 4, Local Demographics.

Bureau of Economic Analysis

Part of the U.S. Department of Commerce's Economics and Statistics Administration, the Bureau of Economic Analysis (BEA; www.bea.gov) produces what it calls economic accounts, which are collections of statistics about the performance of the economy.

The BEA makes it easy to find its local-level sources. Visit the Regional Economic Accounts page on its site (www.bea.gov/ regional) for links to data on regions, states, metropolitan areas, BEA-defined economic areas, and counties. This webpage includes the following key regional BEA resources, which offer data in your choice of charts, graphs, maps, or interactive tables:

- Gross Domestic Product (GDP) by State and
  Metropolitan Area: These economic accounts
  currently break down data from 1998 by industry.

- Local Area Personal Income and Employment:
  Current local-area tables include annual estimates for
  counties, metropolitan areas, and BEA economic
  areas on data such as employment and earnings,
  personal income, and compensation by industry.

- BEA Regional Fact Sheets (BEARFACTS): These
  data sheets, with tables, graphs, charts, and bulleted

lists, compare an area's personal income and gross domestic product with those of the U.S. as a whole.

Chapter 5, Local Economics, goes into more detail about using BEA resources for finding information about local economic conditions.

Bureau of Labor Statistics

The Bureau of Labor Statistics (BLS; www.bls.gov) focuses on labor economics, including inflation and prices, employment and unemployment, pay and benefits, spending and time use, and productivity. You can find local-level sources on the Overview of BLS Statistics by Geography page of this agency's website (www.bls.gov/bls/geography.htm) or through its Geographic Guide (www.bls.gov/guide/geography). The following BLS programs do the best job of covering substate labor statistics:

- Current Employment Statistics (www.bls.gov/ces): Look for detailed industry data on employment, hours, and earnings of workers on nonfarm payrolls for all 50 states, the District of Columbia, Puerto Rico, the U.S. Virgin Islands, and more than 400 metropolitan areas and divisions.

- Local Area Unemployment Statistics (www.bls.gov/ lau): This program produces monthly and annual employment, unemployment, and labor force data for geographic regions and divisions, states, counties, metropolitan areas, and many cities *by place of residence.*

- Quarterly Census of Employment and Wages (www.bls.gov/cew): These tables include data for census regions and divisions, states, counties, metropolitan areas, and many cities *by place of employment.*

- Geographic Profile of Employment and
  Unemployment (www.bls.gov/gps): Look here for
  data about the employed and unemployed, by
  selected demographic and economic characteristics.
  BLS currently breaks down these profiles by regions
  and divisions, 50 states and the District of Columbia,
  50 large metropolitan areas, and 17 central cities.

Read more about using BLS-produced data in Chapter 5, Local
Economics.

SEC Filings: A Treasure Trove of Information

Margaret King, InfoRich Group Inc.

U.S. Securities and Exchange Commission (SEC) filings are
some of my favorite places to look for information about officers of publicly traded companies. They contain lots of interesting bits of information, and the format is specified by the
SEC, so there is some uniformity to the filings.

The *Proxy (DEF 14-A)* is one of the first documents that I
search because it generally includes a brief biography, stock
holdings, and compensation information for each officer of the
company. Often, photos of the officers are included. Proxy
statements are easier to read than financial statements, and
proxy statements include information about related-party transactions. Sometimes related-party transactions will uncover
another company with which an officer has a relationship.

For an officer's stock holdings, I consult *forms 3, 4, and 5.*
While the direct ownership data on these forms is important,
I also like to review the footnotes for additional clues about

an officer's indirect ownership. In the footnotes, I have found information about an officer's trusts, partnerships, family members, and more.

When I am interested in learning more about an officer's compensation, retirement, or termination compensation, I will search *forms 10-K* and *10-Q* and examine *Exhibit 10.* (Exhibit 10 is reserved for material contracts.)

There are several options for searching SEC filings, and my favorite sites include

- SEC website (www.sec.gov): Free, full-text searches for the most recent four years only

- Yahoo! Finance (finance.yahoo.com): No full-text SEC search but lots of free company information in one location

- Morningstar Document Research (documentresearch.morningstar.com): Subscription, full-text searching, Boolean searching, geographic parameters, plus lots of other interesting search features

In 2009, the SEC began phasing in requirements for all publicly held companies to file financial statements using eXtensible Business Reporting Language (XBRL). This is good news for searchers. It will make data more interactive, which will allow searchers to find data faster and easier. It will take a few years to have enough data in XBRL format, but it is worth watching for changes in SEC search interfaces.

Regional, State, and Local Government Resources

Regional, state, and local governments frequently provide more detailed geographically based information than federal sources do, but the data won't necessarily be uniform or consistent across locations—even locations within the same state. More likely than not, you will have to visit the websites for each jurisdiction separately. However, what you lose in the ability to quickly gather and compare information about multiple geographic locations you gain in in-depth and first-hand knowledge. If you have the time and resources to check multiple jurisdictions, or if your research is confined to one area in particular, using regional, state, and local resources is often worth the effort.

With larger budgets and more resources than their smaller counterparts, state and regional governments make good starting points for information about the smaller entities within their boundaries. More and more cities and towns, however, are investing in public information systems—often combined with mapping technology. These data sites are excellent sources for public records, business statistics, and demographics. The Data.gov (www.data.gov) website maps state, local, and tribal data sites at www.data.gov/statedatasites.

When looking for resources from regional, state, and local governments, start with their official websites. As is the case with federal sources, information from local governments can be scattered across various agencies or sections of their websites. Try the site search feature or site map, and look for links to reports, data, or maps. Certain departments, such as planning, zoning, or economic development, tend to collect and use information, and they're usually willing to share it. Many larger jurisdictions have geographic information systems departments, which provide data-mapping services to individuals and businesses. Look around and see what you can find. If you can't locate what you need quickly, look for names of people who might be able to help.

To find official government sites, try entering the keyword *government* with the name of your location in a general-purpose search engine. You can also link to official sites through these directories:

- State and Local Government on the Net (www.state localgov.net)

- USA.gov: Local Governments
  (www.usa.gov/Agencies/Local.shtml)

Economic development agencies, which often are semi-governmental or work closely with a local government, frequently provide useful resources for local-level business research. These agencies are covered later in this chapter, in the section on local organizations.

Cool Tools for Searching Local Government Sites

These resources will help you quickly find relevant information on regional, state, and local government sites:

⇨ GovScan (www.govscan.com): Powered by Google, GovScan searches more than 5,000 city, town, county, and state government websites within all 50 states.

⇨ State Agency Databases (wikis.ala.org/godort/ index.php/State_Agency_Databases): This resource links to databases available on state websites, many of which contain county-, municipal-, and even ZIP code-level data.

Local Organizations

Many local organizations gather and disseminate business and market information, and today most have a web presence. Depending on the size of both the region covered and the organization, you can often find useful statistics, news, and market studies through these organizations. If they're unable to answer your questions themselves, the people within these organizations can usually direct you to experts or other resources. Following are the various types of organizations with a local focus:

- *Chambers of commerce* focus mainly on business issues. Turn to local chambers for company listings as well as demographic, industry, and economic information.

- *Convention and visitors bureaus* are geared toward tourism topics, and their websites often highlight events, places of interest, and general information about a location.

- *Economic development organizations* can be governmental or nongovernmental entities. In either case, their purpose is to attract residents and businesses to a geographic area. In addition to business and market data, try economic development organizations for information about local issues and quality of life.

- *Local chapters of national associations* combine subject expertise with a local focus. Some regularly publish market studies and salary surveys, and the people within these groups generally have in-depth knowledge about their region.

- *Nonprofit organizations* also combine subject and local expertise. In competition for donations, volunteers, and service users, many have increased their market research efforts. Try contacting the people at these nonprofits to see if they're willing to share this information.

Not all organizations are interested in or have the resources for collecting and updating the information you are seeking, and results often vary by location and topic. Also, before you use a group's information, consider its mission. Is the organization focused on providing unbiased, accurate information or promoting the benefits of a particular location?

To identify local organizations, you can try any general-purpose search engine and enter the organization type and location as keywords (e.g., *"chamber of commerce" Seattle*). You can also try these specialized tools, which you can search or browse by location:

- Chamber of Commerce Directory (www.chamberof commerce.com/chambers)

- Economic Development Directory (www.ecodev directory.com)

- Tourism Offices Worldwide Directory (www.towd.com)

- ASAE Gateway to Associations Directory (www.asaecenter.org/Community/Directories/ associationsearch.cfm)

- GuideStar (www2.guidestar.org)

- Idealist.org (www.idealist.org)

Specialized Resources

Several specialized directories, databases, and search engines compile local business content or provide options for geographically based searching. Some of these tools cover both local and nonlocal information, while many offer just local content.

The advanced searching features and specialized content in such fee-based services as LexisNexis (www.lexisnexis.com) and Dialog (www.dialog.com) help you quickly drill down to the local level in business directories and databases. (Several low-cost, fee-based sources and tips for using them to find local information are discussed in Chapter 9, Paying at the Pump.) You can find many free, specialized resources on the web, although they generally lack the full content or features of their premium counterparts. For example, information from data powerhouse Dun & Bradstreet (www.dnb.com) is available through several fee-based services, including Hoover's (www.hoovers.com), LexisNexis, and Dialog. It's also available at no charge through zapdata (www.zapdata.com). While zapdata doesn't have the power-search features of the other products, it works well for counting companies within a particular geographic location or compiling a brief industry overview for a defined area.

For almost any topic, you can find a specialized database, directory, or other search tool that will help you drill down to the local level:

- *People-finding* search engines and directories such as ZoomInfo (www.zoominfo.com), Wink (wink.com), and Pipl (pipl.com) generally allow searching by geography.

- Many tools for finding *images, podcasts,* and *other non-text formats*, such as YouTube (www.youtube.com) and PodcastDirectory.com (www.podcast directory.com), use geotagging and other technologies for location-based searching.

- Find *business* and *market information* through zapdata, ThomasNet (www.thomasnet.com), and YourEconomy.org (www.youreconomy.org). Sometimes, you'll uncover business information where you would least expect it. For example, in addition to real estate listings, Trulia.com (www.trulia.com) devotes a section of its site to ZIP code-level market statistics and trends. At LocalSchool Directory.com (www.localschooldirectory.com), district- and building-level information tell about a location's economic stability and quality of life.

- Some sources specialize in *hyperlocal information*, which generally focuses on community-level areas. Examples include Outside.in (www.outside.in), HelloMetro (www.hellometro.com), and HomeTownLocator (www.hometownlocator.com). In addition to links and guides to local businesses and attractions, they offer articles, blogs, Q & A sections, and online forums. These resources continually add new locations to their collections.

- Specialized databases compile *news*, *journal articles*, *company information*, and *other documents* from multiple sources and add powerful search features for finding documents by location, date, author, and other variables. Public libraries purchase subscriptions to these databases, and residents are permitted to search for and download documents for free. Ask your librarian about these and other specialized tools the library might offer through the web—and be sure to check about the usage rules.

There are so many databases and search tools covering so many topics that it's impossible to list them all in this book. I discuss several excellent specialized resources in Chapters 4 through 8, which include examples of using them for finding information about local demographics, economics, companies, people, and issues.

News Resources

News reports, either from or about a particular location, are a rich source of local information about public and private companies, people, and much more. Local news stories from newspapers and television and radio stations can come in print, web, or audio and video formats. While searching local sources, you might be looking for breaking or current news or taking a look back in time.

You can often find news about a particular location from national sources, but local outlets cover local topics in far greater detail than their national counterparts do. They'll chronicle local events or regional catastrophes long after the national press has moved on to the next story. Local news sources also offer something the larger outlets can't—a local perspective. Knowing what's important to local residents is quite valuable when you're doing geographically based business and market planning. You can also identify local experts by seeing who the local media interview. While the quality, quantity, and availability of local news stories can vary greatly by location, local media do a good job of filling in the gaps left by national sources.

The information you use can have a serious impact on your business, so it pays to use some caution when you're mining news sources for local business and market information:

- Watch for any biases.

- Separate fact from opinion, and know when you should use each.

- Be cautious of errors that can and do occur in news stories on a regular basis.

- Use a variety of news sources to get several sides to a story and to verify facts.

Websites of News Outlets

The websites of newspapers, magazines, and television and radio stations generally provide links to the latest stories and interviews. Some sites even include added content such as podcasts, blogs, and special reports. While a number of news outlets allow free access to all web content, others charge for back issues or limit access to subscribers only. If you're not researching multiple locations, going straight to the local press is a fast, easy route to locally focused news content.

Try some of the following directories for news outlets within a particular geographic region:

- NewsVoyager (www.newsvoyager.com) includes links to newspapers throughout the world.

- American City Business Journals (www.bizjournals. com) publishes business weekly newspapers in more than 40 cities.

- News and Newspapers Online (library.uncg.edu/ news) has links to newspapers and broadcast news outlets offering free access to current, general-interest, and full-text news.

- ABYZ News Links (www.abyznewslinks.com) is composed mostly of newspaper websites from around the world, but you'll also find some broadcast stations, magazines, and press agencies.

- Radio-Locator (www.radio-locator.com) links to webpages and audio streams of private and public radio stations from the U.S. and around the world.

News Aggregators

Aggregators save the legwork by collecting breaking news content—either manually or by machine—from multiple sources and organizing it in one place. Generally, aggregators show a headline and the lead paragraph or a summary, and you click through to the full article on another site.

On Google News (news.google.com), one of the most widely used news search engines, the advanced search page currently allows you to enter a country or U.S. state in the Source Location box to retrieve articles *from* that location. Another option is to enter a city, state, or ZIP code in the Location box, which will retrieve only articles *about* a particular location. Bing News (www.bing.com/news) also offers searching by location.

Several other free sites search and pull together news content, usually organized by topic—and some even filter your news by location:

- Select a U.S. city, state, or ZIP code, and Topix (www.topix.com) creates a continually updated page with news, events, and other information.

- At EveryBlock (www.everyblock.com), you can filter your news to the neighborhood, quadrant, ward, and ZIP-code level.

- Newser (www.newser.com) offers a local news index covering major metropolitan areas (www.newser. com/siteindex/local.html).

- Covering cities and regions in the U.S., the U.K., Canada, Australia, New Zealand, and Ireland, Fwix (fwix.com) deals with topics related to business, crime, sports, politics, and the environment.

- Yahoo! News currently offers a local section (news.yahoo.com/local-news). Select a location, and you're taken to a webpage with the latest news and video.

One thing to remember is that any site that takes you further from the source increases the chances of errors. Many aggregation sites compile news using computer programs, and, for example, they may not pick up any corrected follow-up articles. In some cases, it pays to track the article to its original source. By taking this extra step, you can make sure nothing has been changed in the article that would affect its meaning and importance or would affect any decisions that that will be made based on the content

Social Media Resources

The social media, sometimes called *Web 2.0* or the *social web*, includes blogs, wikis, and sites for bookmarking, file sharing, and networking. The main distinction between social media and some of the other online resources mentioned in this chapter is *human interaction*. Through this human interaction, local information is created, organized, and shared—and much of it is quite useful for business purposes. Businesses are participating in the social web in growing numbers, and serious business researchers have discovered that it is a valuable source for information that won't be found in any static document or site. You can use social media sources to

- Tune in to local issues and consumer opinion

- Track local trends

- Connect with local people

- Find images to get an insider's view of a community

Using the social web for local business research can have its drawbacks. You need to be extremely cautious when it comes to the sources you choose, the information you take from them, and what you do with it. Always add an extra layer of skepticism, and make sure you base critical business decisions on more than just what you gather from sources on the social web.

Another problem with using social media resources is that the noise level is quite high, which means that it's difficult—and often time-consuming—to sort through the junk to find what's really useful. Searching for business-related, localized information from social media is by no means an exact science, and most sites or finding tools don't have any sort of location-based advanced searching.

You can always see what happens if you just add a place-name to your keyword search, but it's pretty much hit-and-miss. A few social media sites and search tools do, however, offer features that can help you search by geography.

The following sections in this chapter cover the current major social-media outlets, what they offer, and some of the ways to extract their local information. Keep in mind that these sources are constantly changing, so be sure to check this book's companion website, ResearchOnMainStreet.com, for updates to these social media resources.

Blogs

Blogs have come a long way in just a few years, and many contain useful business information. Companies blog about their products, and consumers blog about their experiences with companies and their products. Other people post comments to blog posts, adding even more to the conversation. Blogs about places, sometimes called *hyperlocal blogs* or *placeblogs*, contain lots of local perspective and opinion, and they can lead you to local experts.

Blog searching by location, on the other hand, has not developed as far. For example, at this time, Google Blog Search (blogsearch. google.com) and the blog search engine Technorati (technorati.com) don't offer any way to add geography to your search other than using your place-name as a keyword.

Some blog search tools do have geography-based searching, including the following:

- Placeblogger (www.placeblogger.com), a directory of place-related blogs from all over the world, lets you search by place-name.

- At Feedmap (www.feedmap.net), you can browse the list of worldwide locations or search by city, state, or postal code.

- InOtherNews.us (www.inothernews.us) organizes
  U.S.-based news blogs by state.

Twitter

Like blogs, microblogging sites such as Twitter (twitter.com)—
which allows you to provide followers with 140-character
updates—have recently gained the attention of businesses.
Businesses are contributing updates, and researchers are discovering
that useful business information can be found amid the noise. If
you're looking for information from or about a particular location,
then you have the added challenge of searching by geography.

There are several approaches to finding local content on
Twitter, including local events, people, issues, trends, opinion,
and other topics:

- To find tweets *about* a particular location, you can
  enter the place-name in the search box on Twitter's
  main page. It also helps to search the name with the
  hashtag (e.g., *#Denver*) in case anyone has used this
  technique for tracking conversations.

- To search for tweets *from* a particular location, go to
  Twitter's advanced search page (search.twitter.com/
  advanced). There you can specify a place (e.g., name,
  ZIP code) and a surrounding area.

You can also try these sites that search Twitter and are designed
specifically for finding local content:

- Localtweeps (www.localtweeps.com)

- Nearby Tweets (www.nearbytweets.com)

- TwellowHood (www.twellow.com/twellowhood)

- tweetzi Local (www.tweetzi.com/local)

Social Networking Sites

There are sites for online professional networking, and there are sites that are purely social in nature. Both can provide valuable information for business researchers. LinkedIn (www.linkedin. com), Facebook (www.facebook.com), and other social networking sites allow people to set up profiles and participate in virtual conversations. Use these sites to search for experts located within a particular area or to find people who work for local companies or have worked for them in the past. Join location-based groups, and ask people in your network for introductions.

To search LinkedIn, you'll need a free membership. Visit the advanced search page (www.linkedin.com/search), where you can easily search by location. You don't have to be in someone's network to view that person's profile, but it's easier to reach someone if you're connected—either directly or through someone in your network.

You'll also need to register in order to search Facebook, and— at this time—Facebook doesn't have an advanced search page. After you do a basic search, the People search results can be filtered by location. Some people restrict the amount of information they share with those they have not "friended," so it's often difficult to get details.

In addition to searching the major social networking sites by geography, look for location-based, or hyperlocal, social networking sites. These sites focus on connecting people located or interested in a particular place, from the regional to the block level:

- Through Meetup.com (www.meetup.com), you can link with people virtually and meet in person or online.

- Browse or search for cities and neighborhoods in Yelp (www.yelp.com). You'll find discussion lists in the Talk section of your location's webpage.

- StreetAdvisor's forums (www.streetadvisor.com) are organized by state, and people discuss, ask questions about, and share opinions about places.

Content-Sharing Sites

Another part of the social web that can be useful to business researchers, especially for nontext materials, are sites that allow people to share photos, videos, maps, presentations, and other content. Unfortunately, it's fairly difficult to search these sites by location. Again, this is a rapidly changing environment, so what follows are some content-sharing sites and the current options for geographic searching:

- YouTube (www.youtube.com): First enter a basic search, and then narrow it by location.

- Flickr (www.flickr.com): Go directly to the advanced search page, enter your location, and search by tags.

- Google Maps (maps.google.com): Enter your location for user-contributed photos and maps. Click the More Info link and look for the links under Popular Places, which will take you to webpages that compile information about businesses, cities, and points of interest throughout the world.

In Chapters 4 through 8, I show how to use these key resources when you need to find information about local demographics, economics, companies, people, and issues.

Hints for Choosing the Right Resources

⇨ You won't come across one perfect resource. Finding high-quality local business and market information requires a mix of sources.

⇨ Your time is money. When deciding between free and fee-based resources, be sure to include the expense of your time when calculating a source's true cost.

⇨ Take advantage of location-based finding tools to identify news, organizations, governments, specialized sites, and social media that will lead you to insiders' views of cities, towns, and neighborhoods.

⇨ Make sure you're using reliable sources. Read Chapter 3, Avoiding Shady Characters, and learn how to avoid scams, hoaxes, and misinformation.

Endnote

1. Ben Gilad, "My Source Is Better Than Your Source!—The Argument Over Primary and Secondary Sources," *Competitive Intelligence Review* 6, no. 3 (1995): 58–60.

Avoiding Shady Characters: Evaluating Information on the Web

Finding information on the web involves more than just searching and gathering. It also requires making sure you're using the most reliable, accurate, and high-quality information available. In addition to fast, easy access to information, the age of Google has unfortunately brought scams, hoaxes, and misinformation. Information quality is a huge issue for the business researcher because chances are there's a lot on the line—and you can't afford to make costly mistakes.

What's the Problem?

It wasn't a local story, but it's a lesson for all researchers about what can happen when you make decisions based on bad information. In September 2008, a 6-year-old news article about the 2002 bankruptcy filing by United Airlines was, for some reason, still on the website of a Florida newspaper. That day, it was somehow picked up by an automated web crawler, a computer program that scans the web for new content, and was posted with current news. The article was then picked up by the automated systems of other publishers, and people believed that the company had again filed for bankruptcy. This error started a chain of events that caused United's stock prices to plummet that day.

Information quality is an issue for any online business searcher— whether the information is on the global, national, or local scale. When you're looking for local information, however, it's an even bigger concern since good sources covering small geographic areas are hard to find. It's difficult to turn away from a resource when you know you won't find many alternatives; sometimes you have to make do with something that's less than ideal. Just make sure that the information is up-to-date, accurate, and unbiased.

Evaluating your sources and the information they provide requires time, critical thinking, some instinct, and a few simple guidelines. Also, no matter what type of online research you're doing, it helps to know ahead of time what dangers are lurking out there so that you can do your best to avoid them.

Everyone's an Expert

Anyone can call oneself an expert, anyone can post a website, and the rise of the social web has only made the problem worse. Sites frequently don't provide sources, qualifications, or credentials. They make claims that are based on flawed or nonexistent data, and it's essential to separate the counterfeit from the credible.

Ask yourself the following questions when you're deciding whether a site is trustworthy:

- Who is the author, and what are his or her qualifications?

- Does this information come from a reputable publisher?

- Does the author or the publisher provide the sources of the information?

If you can't find the answers to these questions, look for contact information so you can ask someone who is responsible for the site. If a site doesn't offer any contacts, or if no one responds to your inquiry, think twice about using it as a resource.

Everyone Has an Opinion

Frequently, sites that provide "facts" are merely promoting their agenda. Perhaps they're selling something, or they might be trying to convince you to see their point of view. For example, if you're learning about a city from a chamber of commerce or a convention and visitors bureau, it helps to realize that the goal of the site is to promote the city. This doesn't mean that these organizations don't provide useful and accurate information, but you need to make sure you understand a website's purpose and evaluate how it might affect the information.

These questions will help you separate fact from opinion:

- What is the purpose of this site (to inform, persuade, sell)?

- Who sponsors the site, and what's the sponsor's goal?

- Does the information reflect any biases?

- Does it present all points of view or just one side of the discussion?

You Don't Always Get What You Want

It never fails. No matter how carefully you construct your search or select your keywords, at some point you realize that your search results just aren't relevant. You might come across what sounds like a great resource, only to find that it has no in-depth information or doesn't add anything to what you already know. Or perhaps you've bought a market research report or an article, only to find that it doesn't have the information you need. When you're evaluating the usefulness of a document or webpage, learn to scan it quickly for signs of the intended audience and for whether it goes into the detail that your project requires.

These are examples of some of the questions that help determine if a site is relevant to your project and your information needs:

- What topics are covered or not covered?

- Does the site offer any information that other sites don't?

- Who is the intended audience?

- What reading or knowledge level is required to use the information from this site?

Looks Can Be Deceiving

It seems that every day you read about online hoaxes or scams and people who want to steal your identity. Sometimes, parody or satire sites can be mistaken for their authentic counterparts. And finally, you have to deal with what's known as *disinformation*—the deliberate posting or announcement of misleading information meant to throw off competitors or influence opinion.

Inaccurate information isn't always deliberate, but that doesn't make it any less dangerous. The United Airlines case demonstrates that finding one news item listed with other breaking news doesn't guarantee that the item is current. In addition, reporting errors, poor editing, transposed numbers, and any number of other glitches—all totally innocent—can affect data quality. Whether or not it's inadvertent, you can turn up incorrect information in just about any

source, so to avoid being misled or deceived, you need to arm yourself with some facts and some common sense.

Look for answers to the following questions when you're checking a site's authenticity:

- Does this information appear to come from a
  reputable source?

- Compared with other findings and what I know about
  the topic, does this information make sense?

- What are the potential problems with how this
  information was gathered, analyzed, or delivered?

- What do others say about this site or resource?

The Timing Isn't Always Right

It's difficult to find current facts and figures on the web—especially
for small geographic areas. Local-level survey results usually come
last in the reporting cycle, and they're often updated with less frequency than the results for larger geographic entities. Information
may not be reported consistently, making it difficult to make comparisons or spot trends. Another challenge is determining whether the
content on a website is current or outdated. The news article about
United Airlines that was inadvertently picked up years after it was
actually published may have sounded credible, but there was no date
on the article, which should have tipped off a good researcher.

Ask these questions when it comes to checking for problems with
timeliness:

- Is this information current, or does it cover the
  appropriate historical period?

- Are links on the site working, or are they out of date?

- Does the site include outdated articles?

- When was the last update?

They Don't Make It Easy

Some sources might be packed with just the right kinds of information for your research. Unfortunately, there are times when an information source is so difficult or time-consuming to use that you wonder whether it's worth the effort to familiarize yourself with it. Some information sources require specialized software, or they might involve a steep learning curve. The information publisher may put limits on whether and how you can share the information with others. Because of the way information producers package their data, it's often difficult to compare findings across several locations or identify trends over time. For most business searchers, time is money; unless you plan to become a regular user of a particular source, it usually doesn't make sense to spend much time learning all its special features.

These questions will help you evaluate a source's usefulness:

- Is the information well-organized and can you quickly drill down to just what you need?

- Does the format make the information easy to analyze, use in reports, or send to others?

- Do graphics or other special features delay your research by making pages load more slowly?

- Do you need to download or learn how to use special software to access the information?

- Is the information worth your time and effort?

Now that you know what to expect, how can you work around the issues involved with online information?

Tips for Finding Quality Local Information

While some websites are dangerous or just offensive, many contain excellent local-level information. It's worth the effort to find the good websites, and the following tips will help make the trip go more smoothly.

View All Sources With Skepticism

When working with business and market information, there's a lot at stake, and it's always best to be skeptical of what you find online. When businesses, money, or reputations are at stake, view any new information source as under suspicion. Always make sure to base your business decisions on high-quality, reliable information.

When looking for sources that go to the local level, you're sometimes limited—and it's tempting to take whatever you can find when you know you don't have many options. There are times when you might have to relax your standards because there isn't much covering your topic or geography. Just be sure to consider that there are limits to how the information should be used and in what context. When sharing with others, be sure to explain any issues with the source.

Use Trusted Sources

While you always need to be skeptical of the information you find online, it helps to develop a list of trusted sources—those you can count on to have good information. If you research a particular topic on a regular basis, you'll eventually become familiar with the respected sources in the field. Look for sites recommended by trusted colleagues, and bookmark those you've found useful.

Librarians, subject experts, and others often create web directories, collections of pre-screened resources. You can generally search the directories or browse by topic. Both Google Directory (directory. google.com) and Yahoo! Directory (dir.yahoo.com) include a Regional subject heading, and you can drill down to the local level. The number and quality of local resources varies geographically.

Thinking About What You Find Online

Robert Berkman, The Information Advisor

When you locate the information you need on the web, how do you determine whether it is accurate and credible? Here are some tips and strategies based on the kind of research you are doing, as well as general evaluation strategies that can apply to all sources you uncover online:

- When you find information about a company's sales, number of employees, balance sheet, or other particulars, always check the timeliness of the data. Too often this kind of information is outdated. Sometimes the best place for credible, timely data about a company is the company itself: Check the About Us or Investors pages on its website. If you can't find any useful information on the website, email or call the company's public relations office.

- Sites for job hunters, such as Glassdoor.com (www.glassdoor.com), often include discussions of the workplace culture and what it's like to work at the company. You can use these sites to get insider-type information about a firm. Take what you find in these community sites with some grains of salt, though, and don't rely on a single review. You can often get a sense of the credibility of the reviewer simply from the manner and style of the writing.

- Job titles and email contacts are often inaccurate. This information is hard to come by and may be outdated since people change jobs often. Never assume the information is correct. Sometimes the best way to get a person's company email address is to use the most common email format at a company (e.g., last name.first initial@companyname. com). At worst, it will be returned to you. At best, you'll have reached the person you are trying to reach.

- ZoomInfo (www.zoominfo.com), Pipl (pipl.com), 123people.com (www.123people.com), and other aggregation sites scour the web and automatically piece together information about people. These resources can turn up good data but can also be misleading by providing information that seems to be about one person or company but is actually about others.

- Consumer review sites such as Yelp (www.yelp.com) can be helpful, but you should remain skeptical. Does a positive review sound as if it was written by a marketing person for the site? Is something so negative that it sounds hard to believe? The best thing to do with these sites is to look for a general pattern—something mentioned by many people—and always use more than one consumer review site.

- Wondering about Wikipedia (www.wikipedia.org)? The statements made in Wikipedia are most credible when they have an accompanying footnote at the bottom of the page to document the original source. You can sometimes glean insights into a Wikipedia entry by clicking on the Discussion page to find out the story behind the information in an entry. When in doubt, consider what you find on Wikipedia as a lead, and look to see if you can verify it with another source (one that does not cite Wikipedia as its source!).

You can also visit the websites of local public or college libraries as they often contain directories of resources—hand-picked by librarians—with local information. You may also find links to resources from local chambers of commerce, convention and visitors bureaus, and economic development organizations. When trying to track down trusted sites, always ask yourself who would care enough about this topic to have taken the time to evaluate and collect the best resources.

The sites mentioned throughout this book have been carefully reviewed and tested, and while everyone's situation and research questions are different, the sources and techniques described in this book make good starting points for local research.

Verify What You Find

Never, ever rely on a single source. Even the most trusted sources make mistakes, and in business, even the slightest error can be costly. Take these steps to verify what you find:

- Check several articles, look at different data sets, and consult a variety of sites.

- Compare the information you find, and look for discrepancies.

- Look for a list of references, follow links whenever possible, and verify that the author or publisher has accurately quoted from the source.

- Was anything omitted that could change outcomes or decisions?

While you're online, watch for experts who can help verify the information. Who is posting articles or presentations about the topic? Whose name comes up when others talk about this subject? Have you identified an association that specializes in your area of interest? Check the investor relations, corporate communications, and management sections of corporate websites to identify people who might provide additional information.

Always make an attempt to verify information. If for any reason you can't confirm what you've found, the decision about whether to use the information depends on what you intend to do with it. Unverified demographics, for example, might be adequate to get a general idea of an area's population. On the other hand, you wouldn't want to use them to determine where to locate your new business.

Whenever Possible, Go to the Source

The further you get from the original source, the more likely that the information contains errors or has been distorted. The more that information is processed, the more it can be altered, as in the following ways:

- Typographical errors change the data.

- Editing processes change the context.

- Added opinions change the content.

These changes can be unintentional or intentional and caused by humans or machines. In the case of the 6-year-old news article about United's bankruptcy filing, automated search crawlers appear to have started and perpetuated the problem. How much financial damage could have been averted if someone had taken the time to check whether United had something on its own website about such a big event? Machines and automated processes remove common sense and intuition—two critical factors in information evaluation.

Scan the articles you're reading for clues about where the authors are getting their information. Do they name the study from which they are quoting statistics? Are references included at the end of the articles? Scan all parts of a website, especially the About Us or FAQ sections, for sources. If sources are not clear, find contact information and ask someone responsible for the content of the website.

Once you've identified the sources of the information in the articles, search for the source names to see if they're available online. Specialized business search tools such as Biznar (www.biznar.com), BNET (www.bnet.com), and even the fee-based databases could speed up the search. On occasion, I have successfully secured original articles and reports by calling or emailing the author or publisher.

At times, as in the case of a press release about a market research report in which snippets of data from the report appear, it might be cost-prohibitive to go to the original source; you may have to settle for the figures quoted in the press release. It still pays, however, to track the report down and, at the very least, make sure it comes from a reputable publisher.

See What Others Think

When determining the value of a particular resource, it's useful to read reviews or comments others have made about it. Has anyone else used it as a source? You can also learn a lot about a resource by identifying other sites that link to it. Well-regarded sources, including government agencies and nonprofits, frequently include lists of recommended online resources. Bloggers link to other bloggers in their "blogrolls," and respected authors quote other respected authors.

You can see what others think about a particular resource by using these methods:

- Enter the name of the entity or the title of the resource into a couple of general search engines. Visit webpages that mention the resource in question. Is it a favorable or not-so-favorable mention? Who is making the referral, and can he or she be trusted?

- Copy the resource's URL. On the Google advanced search page, paste the URL into the Find Pages That Link to the Page search box. Visit some of the webpages on the results list to see if the referring site is a credible source.

If other sites don't link to a resource, if you can't find any reviews, or if no one has used it as a source, it's important to explore why and consider whether it's worthy of mention.

Get Smart

The better you know your topic, the easier it will be to find quality information. Even if you're not a subject expert or don't research a particular topic or region on a regular basis, getting up to speed doesn't have to take a lot of time. Here are some ways you can become a smart information consumer:

- Use a general-purpose search engine to find sources that will help you learn the fundamentals of your topic.

- Get acquainted with some basic terminology and definitions.

- Pull some background information on your target location or locations from city, county, and state websites and the sites for chambers of commerce, economic development organizations, and local associations.

- If you're working with statistics, make sure you have an understanding of basic data-collection and reporting principles.

When getting background on a particular location, don't limit yourself to just web resources. Your best information could come from a local resident. Use the web to identify who might be both knowledgeable and willing to spend a few minutes talking with you. Read more about gathering information from people in Chapter 7, Looking for Locals.

Finally, if you want to stay informed and monitor your topic, some technology tools may save you time. Set up alerts, RSS feeds, or use Yahoo! Pipes (pipes.yahoo.com/pipes) to track trusted sources and have relevant articles and news releases delivered to your desktop.

Know How to Spot and Avoid a Scam

The dangers of the internet have been well-documented and will always be with us. People who spread deception on the web have become quite sophisticated, and their sites now appear authentic. So how do you defend yourself and avoid the scams, hoaxes, misinformation, and other online hazards? Again, your best defense is to arm yourself with some knowledge. Become a cautious—and educated—information consumer.

To learn more about spotting and avoiding online scams, hoaxes, and misinformation, I recommend you read Robert Berkman's book, *The Skeptical Business Searcher* (Information Today, Inc., 2004). It offers a healthy dose of facts and emphasizes that something else is needed when you're trying to avoid scams: common sense. So remember to stay alert, ask questions, and use your common sense when searching the web for local-level business information.

Checklist for Evaluating Information From the Web

Use a checklist to simplify the process of evaluating online information. You can create your own or adapt this checklist to your needs.

When evaluating websites, look at five criteria:

⇨ Accuracy

- Where do the sites get their information?

- How does the information compare with what you already know?

- Do the sites provide contact information?

⇨ Authority

- What are the author's qualifications?

- Does the information come from a reputable publisher?

- Who links to this site, and what do they say about it?

⇨ Objectivity

- Does this site reflect a particular bias?

- Who sponsors the site?

- What is the purpose of this site? To inform? To persuade? To advertise?

⇨ Date

- Is this information current, or does it cover the period that interests you?

- When was the last update?

- Scan news articles, white papers, and other documents for publication dates.

⇨ Coverage

- Is this site relevant to your topic?

- Does it provide any new information?

- Who is the intended audience, and what level of knowledge is needed for its use?

LOCAL DEMOGRAPHICS

Some of the most frequently asked questions in business and market research are related to demographics. In this chapter, you'll learn where to go when you need current information about people on a very local level, using government data products and other web resources.

About Local Demographics

Demographics are statistics on the characteristics of human populations and population segments. In general, the term *population* refers to a group of people in a particular geographic area, but it can also refer to groups of consumers.

Demographics tell you not only the number of people in a particular location but also about those people, including age, race, gender, marital status, education, and income. Local demographics provide the framework for understanding a particular group of people and answer those business questions that usually begin with "How many?"

Demographic information is used in government, marketing, and opinion research. If you're creating a business plan, local demographics will tell you the size and other characteristics of your target market. When allocating resources, identifying locations for buildings or businesses, or marketing your products and services, you'll need to research demographics—very often for substate geographic areas.

The good news is that a lot of local-level demographics can be found on the web. More and more, you'll find government agencies and other sources posting data sets on their websites and allowing the public to generate customized tables and maps for small geographic entities.

You'll also find that the data is not always consistent across locations, making comparisons more difficult. For example, income or age ranges can vary from source to source. Some states may break down their statistics to county or city levels, while others may not.

In addition, it's hard to tell which resources contain local-level demographics and which do not. Finding the right local demographics for your project is sometimes a hit-and-miss process. For example, the Statistical Abstract of the United States (www.census.gov/compendia/statab) is a vast collection of demographic information. A few tables include data for selected metropolitan areas, but you have to scan the lists of tables in each section of the site to find those that do. Web directories, sites that point you to likely sources, generally don't include clearly marked sections for local information, as they often do for international statistics. For a more focused approach to local business research that won't eat up time or budget, you'll need to know the following:

- The best sites for local-level demographics

- The types of data they provide and what it tells you

- The best strategy for getting to the right demographics at the right time

Before You Get Started

The good news is that you don't have to be a demographics expert in order to extract from the web the local-level statistics that you need. Start by becoming familiar with a few basics of demographics, including definitions, types of demographic information, and geographic boundaries.

Kinds of Information

What kinds of information does demographic data provide? Keep in mind that content and formatting options vary from source to source. Here is a list of some of the variables, or the different ways that population data is broken down, in demographic sources:

- Size
- Geographic distribution
- Age
- Gender
- Marital status
- Race
- Ethnicity
- Household/family size and types
- Transportation/spending habits
- Religion
- Income/wealth/poverty
- Education
- Birth/death rates
- Occupation/industry

- Employment status (self-employed, full- or part-time, unemployed, retired)

- Mortality/morbidity rates

- Disease prevalence

In addition to statistics about people, you will find demographic data on businesses, including total numbers, types, revenues, and other information. Sources for business demographics are covered in detail in Chapter 5, Local Economics.

Types of Data

You'll find several kinds of demographics, differentiated by the time frame they cover:

- *Historical data* looks back in time. Depending on the detail of the data, you may be able to make estimates or projections based on historical trends.

- *Current data* offers a snapshot of the present situation. Be sure to check the date of collection; often the most current data is actually a few years old.

- *Projections* look at the future. Sometimes called *forecasts* or *outlook*, projections use extrapolation and other tools to combine historical and current figures with estimates of the impact of selected outside influences.

- *Estimates* approximate current and past numbers. Estimates use extrapolation tools and outside factors to approximate demographics of the population since the last census.

- *Time series* include data for the same variable at regular points in time, such as how the median age of the population of a city has changed over time. When comparing data, check that time intervals match.

Projections and estimates have their limitations, and using them in your business decision making carries some risks, especially when you're looking for local information. These numbers—even in cases with the most carefully applied demographic principles and methods—are educated guesses. Because of their small sample size, projections and estimates also tend to be less accurate for smaller geographic areas and populations.

Census vs. Survey

A *census* is used to collect population-wide counts. The best known of this type is the every-10-year U.S. Census, which aims to count everyone in the country. Because of the logistics and resources required for these comprehensive studies, they are not done very frequently, and therefore the data becomes dated before the next census is conducted.

A *survey*, on the other hand, gathers data from a small sample of the population and is generally considered to represent the whole. Surveys can provide more up-to-date figures, but you have to assume that what applies to a subset also applies to the entire population. As always, it's important to think of your goals and consider the source. Also take a look at the survey's sample size and how the survey was implemented.

Sometimes, however, you need local-level demographics that are more current than the last census or you want to get an idea of what they'll look like in the future. For example, your investors may want to know if there will be enough people in your targeted demographic to continue supporting your business through the next five to 10 years. Projections and estimates have their uses. Just be sure you know what you're getting, and turn to sources that explain their methodology.

Demographics and Geography

Before you search for local demographic information, it helps to have a basic understanding of how geographic entities can be defined. There are two types of demographic geographic areas: administrative and statistical. Administrative areas are defined by law and include states, counties, cities, towns, and other places. Statistical areas are created by government agencies or other bodies for the purpose of breaking down data. For example, the U.S. Census Bureau has, for reporting purposes, designated census blocks, block groups, tracts, divisions, and other geographic units. *Metropolitan areas*, groups of counties with at least one urbanized area of 50,000 or more inhabitants, are defined by the U.S. Office of Management and Budget and are applied to Census Bureau data. *Micropolitan areas*, created after the year 2000, have at least 10,000 inhabitants but fewer than 50,000.

Statistical areas can change, and it's important to keep that in mind when making comparisons. For example, in 2000 the distinctions between urban and rural areas were redefined, so it's difficult to compare data from earlier censuses. Metropolitan statistical areas periodically change, and new designations can been created. When you're considering using demographics, be sure to check your sources' geographic definitions.

For more information about demographics and geography, go to the U.S. Census Bureau's website (www.census.gov) and click the Geography link. Also, lists and maps of current metropolitan and micropolitan areas and their component counties are provided at www.census.gov/population/www/metroareas.

Decision Points

What path should you take in your search for the right information, and what are some of the decisions you'll have to make along the way? An effective search strategy for local demographics—no matter what type—includes a few basic decisions and steps.

First, you need to know exactly what you're looking for, and it's important to take time for this step before you start your search. Be very clear about what geographic area or areas you're studying. Consider the required time frame. Do you want historical, current, or forecast numbers? Will estimates do, or do you need exact counts? For what variables, or details about the people within the study area, are you searching? Finally, decide on some alternatives. What demographic data would be sufficient in case you can't find exactly what you need?

Take a look at your sources and make sure you know how and when the information was gathered, which will give you a better picture of what the numbers actually reflect and will help you determine whether a source matches your needs and expectations. Any reliable source will reveal the methodology it used. If a source doesn't provide this information, look for contact information so you can ask the author or publisher.

You probably want up-to-date numbers when you're sending your business plan to possible investors. For background information to be used in an internal company report, however, older numbers might be good enough. Are you sizing a market because you want to get a general sense of its potential, or are you preparing to make expenditures based on the data? If you can't find demographics for the ZIP-code level, what other levels would work? Several factors come into play when considering what's "good enough," including how the demographics will be used, who needs them, and the budget and time frame.

Although broad demographic information is quite plentiful, especially from the U.S. government, free, customizable tables for smaller geographic areas can be difficult to find. Consider what your time is worth and whether it might be more cost-effective to purchase demographic reports rather than try to compile them yourself. Nielsen Claritas, for example, offers some low-cost products (www.claritas.com/MarketPlace/Default.jsp), and citing a Claritas report—or one from another recognized provider of demographics—often adds credibility to your research results.

Chapter 9, Paying at the Pump, goes into more detail about using fee-based sources to find demographic information, including when to consider their use.

Best Places to Look

Local demographic information can be found in both national and local sources. National sources supply data for the nation, states, counties, cities, or other geographic areas. Local sources generally provide demographics for just their region.

Using national sources is easier than going from source to source if you need information about more than one location or if you want to make comparisons. However, not all national sources take their data to the local level, and—even when they do—it's not always easy to get to. For example, if you go to the website for the National Center for Health Statistics (www.cdc.gov/nchs), it's not clear which links will take you to local-level data, and you have to click through all of them to make that determination.

Local sources, on the other hand, remove most of the doubt, and they often provide information that can't be found through national sources. Resources that focus on a particular location sometimes are more in-depth and cover topics more relevant to that location. You lose the convenience of being able to research multiple locations through one source, however.

Become familiar with the most up-to-date national sources that include local data, and identify the fastest and most reliable ways of searching local sources.

U.S. Census Bureau

The U.S. Census Bureau (www.census.gov) is the largest producer of demographic information, and it is the primary source of population statistics. On the local level, the Census Bureau provides estimates as well as current and historical figures. Projections are offered on the national and state levels.

The Census Bureau's main undertaking is the U.S. Census, which collects population and housing data every 10 years. The agency also conducts nearly 100 other surveys and censuses every year, and these provide data that's more current than the decennial census. The Census Bureau offers its data in many products and through several websites. Even for an expert researcher, it can be daunting to navigate the various sources and interfaces—especially if you're trying to determine which ones include local data. Here are several sites that contain localized, up-to-date demographics for business and market researchers.

American Community Survey

The American Community Survey (ACS; www.census.gov/acs/www) provides the most current community-level population estimates. It surveys about 3 million households each year and collects information about age, race, income, commute time to work, home value, veteran status, and other variables. Starting in 2008, you can get one-year estimates for selected geographic areas with populations of 65,000 or greater, and three-year estimates are provided for selected areas with populations of 20,000 or greater. A new product, with five-year estimates, was released at the end of 2010 (for more about the differences between one-, three-, and five-year estimates, go to www.census.gov/acs/www/guidance_for_data_users).

The best way to get to ACS results is through the American FactFinder website at factfinder.census.gov. You can view tables, maps, and narratives for counties, congressional districts, school districts, place-names, and other localities. American FactFinder allows you to download data for up to 7,000 geographic areas, which makes it a powerful tool for identifying, for example, places with the most people older than 65.

There are so many options for displaying ACS data that it can be very time-consuming to click through all of them. I recommend following the link for Data Profiles, where you can select your geographic area from a list, click a map, or search by location name or address. For each location, you get five separate statistical profiles:

- Social: education, marital status, relationships, fertility, grandparents

- Economic: income, employment, occupation, commuting to work

- Housing: occupancy and structure, housing value and costs, utilities

- Demographic: sex and age, race, Hispanic origin, housing units

- Narrative: text profile with graphs

Keep in mind, however, that these are not exact counts. The demographics provided by the ACS are estimates, and it's important to note that the smaller the location, the less accurate the estimate—especially in the case of three-year estimates. They are, however, based on reliable data, and in some cases it's the only information of its type available. Again, you need to weigh the pros and cons of using estimates for very local-level demographics.

Population Estimates Program

The Population Estimates Program (www.census.gov/popest/ estimates.html) publishes estimated population totals for the previous year for cities and towns, metropolitan areas, counties, and states. For selected geographic units, estimates are available by age, sex, and ethnicity. While the ACS also generates estimated population and housing data, the Population Estimates Program produces and disseminates the *official* estimates of the population for the nation, states, counties, cities, and towns, as well as estimates of housing units for states and counties.

The estimates are released during the course of the year, in increasing geographic detail, according to this schedule:

- Winter: U.S. and states

- Spring: counties, metropolitan areas, and micropolitan areas

- Summer: cities and towns

The best route to Population Estimates Program results is through American FactFinder, where you can create tables or view the information on maps. Also try the Geography option on American FactFinder's search page.

Small Area Income and Poverty Estimates Program

The Small Area Income and Poverty Estimates Program (www. census.gov/did/www/saipe) was created to provide estimates of selected income and poverty statistics that are more current than those from the decennial census. These estimates are broken down for school districts, counties, and states, and tables and maps can be downloaded from the program's site.

For school districts, in addition to general population numbers, you can find how many children are living in each district and the number of children in poverty living in the district. For the state and county data, this resource provides median household income and breaks down numbers for people living in poverty (by age ranges).

Other Census Products

Also consider these resources from the Census Bureau:

- USA Counties (censtats.census.gov/usa/usa.shtml): While going only as local as the county level, USA Counties offers a quick way to search for information about a wide range of topics, including age, agriculture, ancestry, banking, building permits, business patterns, crime, earnings, education, elections, employment, government, and health. Data comes from the U.S. Census Bureau, the Bureau of Economic Analysis, the Bureau of Labor Statistics, the Federal Bureau of Investigation, and other federal agencies. For a handy overview of county data, try the General Profile table option.

- County and City Data Book (www.census.gov/statab/ www/ccdb.html): The County and City Data Book contains more local statistics than you'll find in USA Counties, but the numbers are not as current. Data is compiled from the Census Bureau and other government agencies for all U.S. states, counties, and cities with a population of 25,000 or more.

- State and Metropolitan Area Data Book (www. census.gov/compendia/smadb): With more than 1,500 data items for the nation, states, counties, and metropolitan areas, the State and Metropolitan Area Data Book is worth a look, although it isn't as current as other sources.

Finding Local Population Data

Peggy Garvin, Garvin Information Consulting

Looking for current local population data for the U.S.? The Census Bureau's American FactFinder is the place to go first:

- In a change from past practice, the 2010 decennial census collected only basic information on age, sex, race, and homeownership status for each person in the U.S. The decennial data is reported at each geographic level, from the smallest (block) to the largest (nation).

- ACS provides estimates of detailed demographic data such as income, education, and housing costs. The ACS data is aggregated for one-, three-, and five-year cycles; only the five-year estimates include all geographic areas down to the block level.

- To protect respondents' privacy, some block-level data may be suppressed in the decennial census reports and especially in the ACS sample-based estimates.

- Statistics from the decennial censuses are not directly comparable with statistics from ACS, because one is derived from a single, full count and the other from ongoing surveys.

Other U.S. Government Agencies

In addition to the Census Bureau, several other federal agencies offer localized information that can be used for business. As with other sources of demographic information, it is a matter of going to the website of each agency to see what it offers and whether it breaks the data down to the local level. Once at the agency site, look for links to statistics, research summaries, reports, or something similar. Here are some agencies and resources that I've found useful for topic-specific local research:

- U.S. Department of Education (www.ed.gov): For demographic-related statistics, go to the Department of Education's School District Demographics System (nces.ed.gov/surveys/sdds). This site is a source for demographics, social characteristics, and economics of children and school districts. You can get quick snapshot reports, create maps, or select tables to compare school district-level data from the ACS and the latest decennial census.

- Social Security Administration (www.socialsecurity. gov/policy): Several resources from the Social Security Administration contain local-level demographics about program recipients. Click on By Subject under Research and Analysis, and then click on the link for Geographic Information.

- U.S. Department of Veterans Affairs (www.va.gov): The Department of Veterans Affairs publishes official estimates and projections of the veteran population and its characteristics through the National Center for Veterans Analysis and Statistics (www.va.gov/ vetdata). In addition to the nation and the states, it offers data for counties and congressional districts. These local-level tables are not as detailed as those for larger geographic areas. For example, they might use fewer and broader age or income ranges.

- Internal Revenue Service (www.irs.gov): Part of the Department of Treasury, the Internal Revenue Service (IRS) site includes useful local data in its Statistics of Income. From the IRS homepage, follow the link for Tax Stats and then click Individual Income Tax. On this page, scroll to the section for Individual Data by Demographic Areas. If you need information that goes below state level, take a look at the county income data. ZIP code tables are available for a fee.

State and Local Government Sources

In addition to federal resources, you can turn to resources from state and local governments. In an effort to bring business and residents to their area, local governments frequently share demographics and other data online. Also, most states will break their numbers down to local levels. These state and local resources are more focused on their region than are resources from the U.S. government, and you don't have to search or browse several data sets to find your specific geographic location.

The time you make up in focus, however, can be quickly diminished by a lot of trial and error since coverage across state and local sites is far from uniform. Some entities may conduct their own surveys, others post data from the U.S. Census Bureau, and still others provide no demographics at all. Your best approach is to use state and local sources when you're researching one or two geographic entities rather than several.

Start with the state or local government's official website. You can use GovEngine.com (www.govengine.com) for finding any type of federal, state, and local government site, or you can go to State and Local Government on the Net (www.statelocalgov.net) for states, counties, and cities.

Once you get to a local government's official website, you'll have to root around because demographics could be anywhere. Use the site's search feature and look up *demographics*, *data*, *statistics*, or other relevant keywords. Look for a list of state agencies or departments. Local affairs and planning departments generally compile and track demographics, and occasionally you'll even come across a state demographer.

Local Organizations

On the local level, several types of nongovernmental organizations publish demographic data in order to attract people and companies to their region, county, city, or town. While you may not be planning to relocate, try looking to the following organizations for strategic business information:

- Chambers of commerce: Depending on the size of the organization and the geographic location, you can usually find data, statistics, or other resources.

- Economic development organizations: These could be private or government groups.

- Convention and visitors bureaus: The people who run these private or government entities are trained to direct people to the right resources.

- Trade groups: Marketing, manufacturing, agricultural, and other professional and promotional organizations collect data on their local markets.

Nothing is uniform when it comes to local organizations, so you'll have to browse or search these sites to find what you need. Look for both people and web-based resources. Chapter 2, Packing the Essentials, covers more about local organizations, including how to find them.

Putting It Into Action

The following three sections include examples of local research projects, covering income and education, health, and historical demographics. For each, I give an example of a reason the information might be needed and the strategy and resources used to find it. While you may not find yourself in these specific situations or asking the very same questions, you can apply the lessons learned to other types of projects.

Income and Educational Levels

Kimberly owns a successful fast-casual restaurant and is thinking about extending her line to a new type of food service: catering teen parties. Her research tells her that this will most likely succeed in an area with higher-than-average income and educational levels. How can she determine whether her city will support this type of business? Kimberly decides that she needs current income and educational figures, as well as some projections that would help her get a glimpse of her community in the future.

She heads for the Census Bureau's website and eventually clicks her way through to a list of links to Census resources, organized by topic (www.census.gov/population/www/popdata.html). By following the Educational Attainment link, she finds that both the ACS and the Current Population Survey (CPS) programs include educational attainment statistics. After reading about each, Kimberly decides to go to the ACS since it has local-level numbers, whereas the CPS covers the national and state levels only.

Through the link provided, Kimberly goes to American FactFinder. There she is able to create customized tables and charts from ACS data. After locating total population projections from the state and city websites, Kimberly realizes that she wouldn't be able to get projected educational attainment levels. Instead, she calculates rough estimates based on the population projections, current population, and current education levels.

Health Demographics

A hospital organization is expanding and, within the next three years, will open three drug treatment centers in the state of Missouri. Andrew, one of the organization's librarians, is asked to provide the site selection team with statistics about drug and alcohol abuse by the residents of several cities and towns within the state. The data will be used to help the hospital locate treatment centers where they were needed most.

Because a quick turnaround is also requested, Andrew realizes he has to focus his efforts and work as efficiently as possible. Rather than taking a location-by-location approach to his search, Andrew decides to start with state resources and see 1) whether they offer drug- and alcohol-related statistics and, if so, 2) how localized the information is. He also chooses to start online but if he doesn't find what he needs in 15 minutes, to identify and make a call to the appropriate state agency.

Andrew starts with the state's official website, which he finds at State and Local Government on the Net. Through a dropdown menu, he goes to a list of state agencies, which link him to the site for the Department of Health and Senior Services. Not quickly spotting a link for health statistics, he tries the site search for *statistics*. The second result after Vital Statistics looks just right: Data, Surveillance Systems & Statistical Reports. Following this link, he decides to try Community Data Profiles (state, county, and city profiles). He discovers that these profiles offer a table called Drug and Alcohol Problems. The table offers just county-level figures, but the information for each county is quite extensive. In addition to drug and alcohol usage statistics, the county profiles include the number of people incarcerated for substance abuse consequences, as well as estimates of the amount of substance abuse treatment needed in the county. While Andrew's client didn't ask for this additional information, Andrew decides that it would help the site selection team make a better decision about where to locate the new clinics.

Time is running out, so Andrew decides to present the site selection team with the county-level data. By using Google Maps (maps.google.com), he identifies which counties included the cities and towns listed in the team's initial request.

While scanning the state's website, Andrew finds and bookmarks a list of local public health agencies. He lets the team know that if it still requires city- or town-level data—and if it approves the additional project time—he will call these agencies for help.

Historical Trends

Angela is conducting research for her client, a well-known author working on her next book. The book examines several key events in the state's history and explores their impact on the population in different parts of the state. The author asks Angela to put together pre– and post–World War II population profiles, including age, race, and other factors.

To get a sense of how the demographics had changed after the war, Angela decides to compare 1940 and 1950 county-level census data. She heads to Social Explorer (www.socialexplorer.com), a site she'd previously used to obtain historical U.S. Census results. Using the mapping and reporting tools, Angela is able to put together a profile of the population's general characteristics. She discovers, though, that some of the more detailed data, such as foreign-born place of birth, is available only through the fee-based version.

Angela consults some colleagues and comes across the Historical Census Browser from the University of Virginia Library (mapserver. lib.virginia.edu). This site lets her view data from 1790 through 1960 and examine state and county topics for individual census years over time. Angela pulls the numbers for the remaining data points she needs for her profiles, compiles the information her client requested into a spreadsheet, and adds her summary of what key characteristics of the population had changed during the 10-year period.

More Tips for Local Demographics

▷ Use U.S. government data if you need demographics for several locations or if you want to make side-by-side comparisons.

▷ To save time when using federal government data, take advantage of the Quick Profiles, maps, and other preformatted options at the Census Bureau's American FactFinder website.

▷ Use official state websites when researching several locations within one state. It's worth a call to check for the most recent demographic data.

▷ State libraries often collect and share free local-level demographics. To find official websites, got to the Libweb directory (lists.webjunction.org/libweb) and follow the link for state libraries.

▷ Try GovScan (govscan.com), a local-government search engine. Enter your location or locations with the keyword *demographics* to see what departments or offices provide population or housing statistics.

Local Economics

An essential component of business and market research is learning about local economies. This chapter serves as a guide to local-level information about businesses, industry trends and outlook, the workforce, and other economic topics. It provides some background on economic information and the best resources and strategy for researching economic conditions in small, local areas.

About Local Economics

It doesn't matter if you're part of a global enterprise or a one-person business, information about local economic conditions is necessary for making strategic business decisions. These are just some of the situations in which you would need to research local economies:

- Selecting a location for new businesses, headquarters, or branch offices

- Identifying new geographic opportunities

- Connecting with customers in a particular geographic area

- Identifying an area's top industries or companies

- Learning from the economic successes and failures of similar geographic regions

Many factors contribute to the state of an area's economy. During your research, you'll need to look at data about businesses, industry sectors, consumer activity, and other indicators. It's also important to consider any events that can affect area business and industry, such as natural disasters or mass layoffs. Finally, seek the opinion of experts—those who are knowledgeable about both the geographic location and the economy—to get an idea of an area's economic outlook.

Before You Get Started

Understanding local economies is complex. It involves gathering a variety of statistics, rankings, and other information. You also need to add context to what you've found:

- Does it match what people are saying about the local economy?

- How do the local numbers compare with those for similar communities, the state, or the nation?

- What trends can be determined by changes over time?

- Do the current conditions match predictions for the area? If not, why?

Before getting into specifics about sources and strategy, let's look at the types of information needed for researching local economics and how to put that information into context.

Types of Information

Local economic research requires finding several, often interrelated, key pieces of information:

- Key economic indicators: business demographics; employment and unemployment; business starts, failures, and output rates; wages and earnings; housing starts; measures of local government and other economic statistics

- Key industries: main industries, declining industries or industry segments, areas of growth, production rates

- Key companies: major employers, small-to-large business ratio (see Chapter 6, Local Companies, for more detail about researching local companies)

- Key events: layoffs, industrial accidents that keep people out of work, and other occurrences with local economic impact

Expand Your Horizons

Economic conditions and the information about them cross the boundaries of cities and towns. Local economies are part of larger economic systems, and business and industry within a small geographic area can easily be affected by issues and trends in the nation, state, or region. If the state of a local economy doesn't match that of the surrounding area, what might be the contributing factors or lessons learned? It's impossible to get a complete overview of the economic climate on a very local level without looking at the larger picture.

Define what other geographic areas will help you assess the economy of a particular location, including the nation and states. Look for similar communities in the same region. Compare a city or town in one part of the country with others in a different part of the country that are similar in size and demographics. Make use of resources, especially those from the U.S. government, that display economic indicators of multiple locations.

Look Beyond the Numbers

Don't rely just on economic indicators or other statistics. Looking at numbers alone won't provide the full economic picture and can be misleading. Add sources that will give you richer insights than what you would gain from charts and tables alone:

- Check out local news sources for background information that will add perspective.

- Find out what natural disasters, elections, upcoming legislation, or other issues might affect the local economy. Chapter 8, Local Issues, takes a closer look at events that influence a local area's economy.

- Investigate any inconsistencies you see in the statistics.

- Seek out opinions about the economic outlook of the local area.

- Learn how businesses have been affected by past economic ups and downs, which can add insights into the future.

It helps to talk about the local economy with people such as policy makers, local citizens, journalists, and economic development specialists. They frequently offer insights that can't be found in online sources. For more information about adding people into your research mix, see Chapter 7, Looking for Locals.

Industry Codes

Many sources for business and market information rely on standardized codes for industries and industry sectors. Most of these sources organize businesses and industries by either Standard Industrial Classification (SIC) or North American Industry

Classification System (NAICS) codes, and some—such as Hoover's—use their own codes.

SIC, NAICS, and other codes work well if you're researching distinct industries, such as banking or automobile manufacturing. However, it is difficult to classify many businesses, such as those in multiple industries or a new or emerging industry not yet classified. Also, there's no uniform system for assigning codes, and companies in similar industries often wind up with different codes.

When dealing with industry or business information, you'll need to consider whether searching with industry codes is the most effective way to get what you need. Asking these questions will help you decide:

- How else can the industry you're researching be described? Look for any possible alternative codes to add to your search.

- What are your alternatives to searching with codes? Look for resources that also offer keyword and advanced search options.

- What classification codes are used in your sources? When comparing industry data from different sources, make sure you know what's included and whether the two sources' codes are equivalent.

More information about SIC and NAICS codes can be found at the Occupational Safety and Health Administration website (www.osha.gov/oshstats/naics-manual.html).

Decision Points

With so many facets to researching local economics, it helps to streamline your search. Before deciding on the best sources for your circumstances, take some time to consider several important issues related to your research strategy.

What Numbers Do You Need?

No single number reflects the state of the economy. Several factors, including number of businesses, productivity, wages, employment and unemployment rates, and other business- or industry-related statistics or indicators provide insights into local economies. While a multi-faceted approach to researching local economics is recommended, you won't need to find *everything* there is to know about an area's economy. Any decision about what information to gather usually involves the following steps:

- What economic indicators or other data will give you the best picture of the local economy for your particular needs? If you're considering, for example, pitching a new software product to municipalities, data on local government expenditures could help you narrow your list of targets. A manufacturer's representative targeting energy firms will want some statistics covering area energy-sector performance and a list of the top energy companies in the region.

- What alternatives would suffice, in case you don't find all the indicators on your list? If you can't find 10-year projections for all the places on your list, will five-year projections work instead? If county-wide job turnover rates aren't available, will totals for major job categories make a good replacement?

- Is there any flexibility in your geographic definitions? If city information isn't available, should you use county or metro-area data?

While it's a good idea to give some thought to the kinds of information you need, keep an open mind. It helps to search more broadly, rather than narrow your focus too much. You never know what might turn up in your search, and you could be missing out on something valuable.

Past, Present, and Future

The time frame of a data set is an important factor to consider when using economic resources. In addition to *current* economic statistics, you might be working with *historical* numbers or have a need for *projections* (also called *economic forecasts*), which predict what the economic conditions will be in the months or years ahead. *Time series* data, measured at successive and uniform time intervals, helps compare economic conditions, such as number of establishments or unemployment figures, at certain points in the past.

Take a close look at several other time-related factors as well. Find out when the data was collected—not just when it was reported—to get an idea of how current the numbers actually are. Check the frequency of the reports—is your source reporting weekly, quarterly, or annual outcomes? When looking at time series data for several locations, check that your sources provide information for equivalent periods. Also, economic conditions change quickly, and the most recent data may not accurately reflect the current economic situation. As an example, the late-2007 recession altered many forecasts, and sources may not include updates.

It's important to note that for smaller geographic areas, finding specialized economic information such as historical data or projections will be difficult, at least if you rely solely on free resources. Without using one of the premium information sources, you'll find that ferreting out specialized data is often a time-consuming process, generally requiring that you visit the sites of a number of local governments, organizations, and other sources. If you can't find projections for your geographic target, or if you're researching multiple locations, consider using fee-based sources (covered in detail in Chapter 9, Paying at the Pump). These services generally wind up saving you a considerable amount of time.

Let Others Do the Work

Use sources that will give you the best return for your investment in terms of your time and the direct research expenses. The more you can extract from a single source, for example, the quicker you'll work. Here are some ways to let others do the work and get the most out of your research efforts:

- Look for information products that display data in formats that facilitate analysis.

- Whenever possible, use sources that cover multiple locations, to save you the time of having to go to numerous sources.

- Take advantage of handy preformatted webpages or documents with selected indicators for one location, sometimes called *economic quick profiles*.

- Look for sources that show trends over time, including time series data or tables that combine past, current, and projected numbers.

- Know where to go for news, statistics, or other economic information that has been gathered from several sources and combined into one resource.

- Set up alerts to keep up with events or trends that can affect local economies.

Best Places to Look

Federal and local governments, news and business publications, universities, research institutes, and specialized sites can all help you find the pieces needed for understanding local economic conditions. The sites in the following sections include specific sources for local economic information—plus when and how to use them.

U.S. Government

Statistics from the U.S. government have always been well-respected because federal agencies are required to follow strict guidelines for collecting and reporting data. Many federal sources provide up-to-date economic data on national, state, and substate levels. Several products include very small geographic entities, such as ZIP codes, census blocks, and school districts. The major government agencies for local economic information include the Census Bureau and the Bureau of Economic Analysis, both part of the U.S. Department of Commerce, and the Bureau of Labor Statistics, under the U.S. Department of Labor.

Census Bureau

The Census Bureau (www.census.gov)—probably more than any other government agency—measures patterns of American lives and business at every level of geography. While this agency is best known for its population statistics (covered in Chapter 4, Local Demographics), the Census Bureau also provides these economy-related statistics:

- Housing: housing types, ownership, costs, occupancy, and so forth

- Business activity: industry size (jobs, sales, value of shipments, etc.), number of companies and establishments, workforce indicators, and measures of business operations (costs, building and equipment investments, imports and exports)

The Census Bureau collects and disseminates these indicators through several programs. From the Census Bureau's homepage, click on the Business & Industry link for a great starting point for local-level economic data. Under the Data by Geography tab, you'll find a table that compares dates and geographic coverage for the available data sets.

Probably the most well-known of the Census Bureau's economic programs is the Economic Census, which you can find a link to on the Business & Industry page. Statistics on establishments across all sectors of the economy are collected every five years and released over several years in increasing geographic detail. This means that by the time they're released, local results are starting to get a little stale.

If you're looking for substate statistics that are more up-to-date than those from the Economic Census, you can turn to several other U.S. Census Bureau economic programs.

The Local Employment Dynamics (LED; lehd.did.census. gov/led/led/led.html) program develops and distributes detailed reports on local-level labor market conditions. LED integrates existing data with specialized reporting tools that make it easy to identify historic, geographic, and industry trends. Under the Data Tools tab, you'll find several resources for mining local statistics on employment, job creation, turnover, and earnings: Community Economic Development HotReport, Quarterly Workforce Indicators, and Industry Focus reports.

Through the County Business Patterns webpage (www.census. gov/econ/cbp), you can view county, metro, and ZIP code data tables. These include number of establishments, first quarter and annual payroll, and employment during the week of March 12. The data excludes statistics on most government employees and jobs such as household employees and the self-employed. You can also get to County Business Patterns results through American FactFinder (factfinder.census.gov). There you will find results for just counties and metropolitan/micropolitan statistical areas from 2004 forward. What you lose in coverage, however, you make up in formatting options such as interactive maps and customized tables.

Building Permits (censtats.census.gov/bldg/bldginfo.shtml), a survey of local building permit officials, currently includes statistics on residential and nonresidential original construction, changes, and demolitions. Municipalities make up the majority of substate permit-issuing jurisdictions, but you'll also find data for counties, townships, and unincorporated towns.

USA Counties (censtats.census.gov/usa/usa.shtml) collects national, state, and county data from the Census Bureau and several other agencies, including the Bureau of Economic Analysis, the Bureau of Labor Statistics, the Federal Bureau of Investigation, and the Social Security Administration. It includes economy-related statistics on topics such as banking, business patterns, education, employment, health, manufacturers, and much more. USA Counties is especially useful for comparing data over time or for several locations.

And finally, there are federal, state, and local governments. A local government's financial health is closely tied to and offers insights into the economic health of a geographic area. The Census Bureau's Federal, State, & Local Governments website (www. census.gov/govs) reports statistics from a variety of programs covering government employment, revenues, expenditures, and more. You can also find results of special-topic surveys (e.g., libraries, criminal justice, and education) and lists of local governments, their structure, and contact information.

Bureau of Economic Analysis

The Bureau of Economic Analysis (BEA; www.bea.gov) produces collections of national, regional, industry, and international economic statistics. The BEA offers data not found through the Census Bureau or the Bureau of Labor Statistics, including Gross Domestic Product (GDP) figures for states and metropolitan areas. Also, unlike Census Bureau data, BEA data is found on one website, and you can easily track down local-level economic information through one webpage.

From the BEA homepage, click the Regional tab. This page includes a list of state and local BEA programs, including statistics on state and metropolitan GDP and on personal income and employment. You can choose to view BEA regional data sets in interactive tables, charts, graphs, maps, or quick fact sheets.

Bureau of Labor Statistics

The Bureau of Labor Statistics (BLS; www.bls.gov) is responsible for collecting, processing, analyzing, and publishing statistics covering labor economics. You can expect to find the following types of information from the BLS:

- Labor force status

- Job and wage data by place of work

- Prices and living conditions

Most BLS publications cover national data; however, several break their statistics into smaller geographic units. From the BLS homepage, follow the Geography link, and you will find employment, unemployment, and wage information for counties, metropolitan areas, and selected cities and towns. This page also includes a link to the BLS Geography Guide, a handy chart for comparing local coverage of BLS products.

Here are some of the most useful BLS sources for local-level economic data:

- Economy at a Glance (www.bls.gov/eag): These handy tables provide state and metropolitan-area economic profiles, which offer monthly data on the labor force. Follow the Back Data links for historical numbers.

- Local Area Unemployment Statistics (LAUS; www.bls.gov/lau): A federal-state cooperative endeavor, the LAUS program produces monthly and annual employment, unemployment, and labor force data. Geographically, LAUS breaks down the data for census regions and divisions, states, counties, metropolitan areas, and many cities.

- Geographic Profile of Employment and Unemployment (www.bls.gov/gps): This resource provides annual data on the labor force for states and substate areas. It covers selected metropolitan areas, metropolitan divisions, and cities, with sections for historical and current data.

- Consumer Expenditure Survey (CE; www.bls.gov/cex): Collected by the Census Bureau for the BLS, the CE provides information on the buying habits of American consumers. Follow the Geography link to find national, regional, state, and metropolitan-area tables.

- Occupational Employment Statistics (OES; www.bls.gov/OES): With data available for the nation, states, and metropolitan and nonmetropolitan areas, the OES website provides employment and wage estimates for more than 800 occupations.

Other U.S. Government Agencies

Several other federal agencies provide data that is based on geography and focused on a particular topic. The following sections cover six U.S. government agencies and describe their local-level economic information sources.

Department of Agriculture

For many regions, farming and ranching make up a significant portion of the economy. Conducted by the U.S. Department of Agriculture every five years, the Census of Agriculture (www.agcensus.usda.gov) is the only source of uniform, comprehensive agricultural data for every U.S. state and county. Tables report results covering all areas of farming and ranching operations, including production expenses, market value of products, and operator characteristics.

From the Census of Agriculture website, you can get to local-level information by following the links to State and County Profiles; Race, Ethnicity and Gender Profiles; or ZIP Code Tabulations. Another option is to select a state from the pull-down menu on the left side of the page. State pages include state and county reports, county profiles, and congressional district rankings and profiles.

Department of Education

Local economies depend on healthy schools and an educated workforce. The U.S. Department of Education's National Center for Education Statistics (nces.ed.gov) is your best source for local-level educational data, through its Common Core of Data (nces.ed.gov/ccd). Information on schools and school districts can be put into custom tables and downloaded in preformatted reports.

Social Security Administration

The Social Security Administration (www.socialsecurity.gov) provides statistics on topics such as who receives Social Security benefits, earnings and employment data for workers covered by Social Security, and amount of payments broken out by congressional districts. From its main Research, Statistics, & Policy Analysis page (www.socialsecurity.gov/policy), click on By Subject under Program Statistics and Data Files. Once there, you will find a link for Geographic Information. This page takes you to state and local statistical reports.

Federal Deposit Insurance Corporation

An independent agency of the federal government, the Federal Deposit Insurance Corporation offers economic information by geography through its Regional Economic Conditions webpage (www2.fdic.gov/recon). Topics include industry activity, employment and income, and real estate activity. You can create charts, maps, and tables for state, county or metropolitan-area levels; conveniently, these tables display time trends. The data is provided by outside vendors and updated eight times per year.

Federal Reserve Board

The Federal Reserve Board, the central bank of the U.S., publishes the Beige Book (www.federalreserve.gov/FOMC/BeigeBook) eight times per year. This resource summarizes current economic conditions by Federal Reserve District and industry sector. Available in PDF or HTML formats, the Beige Book is a great source of commentary about regional business activity.

For additional regional data, visit the websites of individual Federal Reserve districts. For example, the Federal Reserve Bank of Boston's Indicators Database (www.bos.frb.org/economic/neei/neeidata.htm) covers labor market conditions, home sales, construction numbers, and other statistics for New England as a whole, each of the six New England states, and—for some data series—major New England metropolitan areas. Locate the websites for the 12 local Federal Reserve Districts at www.federalreserve.gov/otherfrb.htm.

Department of Housing and Urban Development

U.S. Department of Housing and Urban Development's (HUD) Office of Policy Development and Research maintains current information on housing needs and market conditions, as well as conducting research on housing and community development issues. Through its USER website (www.huduser.org/portal), this agency offers several data sets with local-level information, including the following:

- American Housing Survey

- Assisted Housing: National and Local

- Fair Market Rents

- Metropolitan Area Quarterly Residential and Business Vacancy Report

- Neighborhood Stabilization Program Data State of the Cities Data Systems

These sources can be found in the Data Sets section of the website. The site's Market Analysis link takes you to Comprehensive Housing Market Analysis reports for HUD-defined Housing Market Areas. Also of interest is the Maps area, which includes additional county-level data in interactive maps.

Where Are the Forecasts?

A lot of analysis goes into producing economic forecasts, which require specialized skills and tools. This means that finding free projections—especially for small geographic areas—can be difficult.

If you're looking for national and state projections, the federal government provides these sources:

➪ The U.S. Bureau of Labor Statistics (www.bls.gov) offers 10-year national employment and occupational projections. From the main page, go to Databases & Tables (www.bls.gov/data) and follow the Employment Projections link.

➪ Congressional Budget Office: Economic Projections (www.cbo.gov/budget/budget.cfm) contains current national economic projections on such indicators as GDP, unemployment rates, consumer price index, tax bases, and much more.

➪ O*Net OnLine (online.onetcenter.org), funded by the U.S. Department of Labor's Employment & Training Administration, provides occupation-related data. Scroll to the bottom of the occupation descriptions to link to state data. These state pages contain 10-year state and national employment trends for each occupation.

For substate projections, visit the websites for individual state and local governments, organizations, educational institutions, and other sources covered later in this chapter. Another option is to use a fee-based source such as Nielsen Claritas (www.claritas.com), which offers its own five-year projections for virtually any geographic location.

State and Local Governments

Although going to separate state and local government sites for the information you need is not very convenient, it's often well worth the effort. Some pieces of local information, such as projections, just aren't found in federal sources.

Scan or search these websites for agencies involved in labor or workforce, economic development, finance, or other economy-related areas of government. Governments vary greatly in how they're organized and the kinds and amount of information they collect and share—so nothing is uniform. Sales and property taxes, for example, can be a useful local economic indicator, but not all states collect these taxes. Some states designate one agency responsible for all topics related to the economy, while others delegate economic issues across several agencies.

Start with state websites before turning to smaller jurisdictions, since many states break down their statistics to the local level. A helpful tool for quickly linking to these official sites is the State and Local Government on the Net directory (www.statelocalgov.net).

Another possible source for government information is the Regional Council of Governments for your area, depending on your specific questions and targeted locations. These geographically based organizations often provide economic data on their websites, and you can find these resources through the National Association of Regional Councils (www.narc.org) site. Just click the Regional Councils/MPOs link.

Local News

The state of the economy is a hot topic, and just about everyone cares about it in some way or another. That's why you'll find lots of articles, opinion pieces, research reports, and other resources about the economy in the news. For information about the local economy, go straight to the local press.

In addition to news about local economies, look for leads to other sources. Who is writing about local economics, and about whom are they writing? What reports or other publications are mentioned in the articles? Area experts, for example, frequently publish reports or updates of local current and forecast economic conditions. These reports are mentioned in news articles or in interviews with the authors. Also, track down the original sources to learn whether additional, unpublished data is available.

You have two options for finding local-level economic news:

- Through the *websites of news sources:* Go directly to the source. Many news outlets include sections on their sites dedicated to the economy. News and Newspapers Online (library.uncg.edu/news) is a directory of links to newspapers and broadcast news outlets. Bizjournals (www.bizjournals.com), the website for American City Business Journals, provides links to its weekly business newspapers, published in 40 cities. Don't forget radio. Find webpages of and audio streams from private and public radio stations at Radio-Locator (www.radio-locator.com).

- Through the *websites of news aggregators:* These specialized sites compile summaries of and links to news articles from many sources. Yahoo! News (news.yahoo.com) and Google News (news.google.com) are two examples of news aggregators that let you drill down to the local level. In Yahoo!, follow the Local link on the main page. In Google, you can enter a location on the advanced search page. Other sites for location-based news include Topix (www.topix.com) and Newser (www.newser.com).

With any type of news search, it's possible that the most useful local information may not show up in print. That's why it's a good idea to scan the news for business journalists, area economists, or other people who could provide additional insights. Tips for tapping into the expertise of local people and preparing for your conversations are found in Chapter 7, Looking for Locals.

Local Organizations

Local organizations and the people within them care about the state of the economy, and they are a great resource for local economic information. Chambers of commerce, economic development groups, and professional associations collect and share data about companies, industry, employment and unemployment, and other economic information. These organizations often are the best source for forecasts and other hard-to-find information. For example, the Metro Denver Economic Development Corporation publishes a summary report on the area's economic forecast for the upcoming year.

You can find the websites of local organizations through search engines, combining place-names with such keywords as *association* or *organization.* Several specialized tools will also help you get to these resources, including the following:

- Economic Development Directory (www.ecodev directory.com): A listing of links to entities, organized by location

- Chamber of Commerce Directory (www.chamberof commerce.com/chambers): More than 7,500 chambers, including contact information and web links

- American Society of Association Executives (www.asaecenter.org/Community/Directories/ associationsearch.cfm): Under the Community tab,

go to Gateway to Associations and search for
relevant associations

At the websites of these local organizations, look for sections
containing publications, statistics, reports, or other documents.
Sometimes you'll come across specific sections of these sites covering the local economy. To focus your search, try the site search
feature or the site map.

Universities and Research Institutes

Whether they are operating independently or in a partnership with
like-minded entities, universities and other institutions often contain
economy-related departments, research groups, or projects. Try the
business schools at the universities in your target locations. Many
business departments host economic forums or house local economic experts and post free reports, articles, or other documents.
Look for published data, or talk with the experts. Find out what
studies they are currently working on and what results, if any, they
are willing to share.

In addition to university business departments, look for groups
that concern themselves with local-area economies. For example,
Research Seminar in Quantitative Economics (rsqe.econ.lsa.umich.
edu), an economic modeling and forecasting unit at the University
of Michigan, publishes forecasts for Michigan and the nation. Some
institutions provide data sources for places throughout the country.
An example is the County and City Data Books website
(www2.lib.virginia.edu/ccdb) from the University of Virginia library,
an excellent resource for extracting historical economic statistics.

In addition to using search engines for identifying academic or
research institutions by location, try these specialized finding tools:

- Economics Departments, Institutes and Research
  Centers in the World (EDIRC; edirc.repec.org/usa.
  html) arranges links by state.

- Peterson's (www.petersons.com) lets you search for college and university profiles by location and specialty.

- The Association for University Business and Economic Research website (www.auber.org) includes a Member Search link.

YourEconomy.org

Christine Hamilton-Pennell, Growing Local Economies, Inc.
YourEconomy.org (www.youreconomy.org) is a useful—and constantly expanding—database created by the Edward Lowe Foundation. It provides information about business establishments in the U.S., tracked across geographic location, industry, and time. The database includes figures on business composition (e.g., how many businesses of a specific size exist in a geographic location or industry), business growth, and specific industry categories.

Data is provided for geographic units that range from the U.S. as a whole to individual counties and metropolitan statistical areas. The data is drawn from the National Establishment Time-Series Database, which is based on Dun & Bradstreet data that is verified for accuracy and augmented to fill in the gaps.

Business establishment data is broken down by noncommercial, nonresident, or resident companies. Data on resident companies is further broken down by stage, or number of employees. You can compare statistics across any period from 2000 forward (e.g., from 2000 to 2008 or from 2005 to 2006), for any geographic location and industry.

I find this resource extremely powerful for uncovering detailed information about local economies. As an example, an economic development specialist might decide to funnel program resources toward services and support for local Stage 2 companies (10 to 99 employees) after learning that in the specialist's county, these companies created 18 percent of the net new jobs in the manufacturing sector between 2006 and 2008 (growth), although they represented only 14.4 percent of all resident establishments within those parameters (composition).

To calculate business growth figures using YourEconomy. org, follow these steps:

- Click on the Growth tab.

- Select a geographic region and/or industry.

- Click the Details link.

- Select the years of interest.

- Divide the number of net new jobs for a given company stage by the total number of positive net new jobs.

This will give you the percentage of net new jobs created by companies within that stage. You can then compare the growth figure to the composition figure (i.e., what percentage of total establishments fall within the selected parameters). Give it a try. It's easier than it sounds!

Putting It Into Action

The following sections provide examples of research projects that involve gathering information about local economics. The strategies and sources used in these examples can be applied to other situations as well. Use them as a guide for your own research projects.

Growth Industries

Becky, a graduate student, has fallen in love with the city in which she is attending school, and she wants to find employment there. The focus of her MBA is business-to-business digital marketing, and she dreams of working in one of the hot growth industries in the region, preferably in renewable energy. She decides to identify the fastest-growing industries and research how the state fares in developing its renewable energy sector.

She heads to the university library website and finds a guide to online economic resources that was compiled by the reference librarians. Through this guide, she links to the LED program from the U.S. Census Bureau. The Industry Focus reports help her rank the top industry sectors in terms of new hire earnings, hiring growth, and employment numbers. The industry sectors are separated according to NAICS codes, but she isn't able to get any specifics about the outlook for renewable energy. None of the listed codes seem to match the industry.

A search of the local weekly and daily newspaper websites, which the student found using a combination of relevant keywords in Google, uncovers several articles about state and local efforts to bring renewable energy businesses to the region. Through one of the articles, Becky identifies someone at the area chamber of commerce with whom she could discuss the energy industry. Through their phone conversation, Becky discovers that the chamber and the city are in negotiations with two renewable-energy firms that are considering relocating to the area.

The LED data helped Becky identify industries in which she could focus her immediate job search. The fact that state, regional, and local entities were teaming up to attract renewable-energy opportunities brought her hope that she might one day work in her desired field and remain in the area.

Labor Force and Unemployment

The executive team of a national manufacturing company wants to explore possible locations for a new plant. Team members have observed that they've had the most success in getting new plants operational quickly in locations with a large pool of unemployed workers within the industry. They ask Daniel, who works in the market research department, to help them identify the most likely cities in the western region of the U.S.

Daniel decides that he needs a source that can tell him about layoffs and unemployment rates by industry and location. He knows that the go-to government agency for labor information is the Bureau of Labor Statistics. At its site, he finds Mass Layoff Statistics (www.bls.gov/data) by industry and by state, but not for smaller locations. He decides to pull the Economy at a Glance profiles for the five states with the most layoffs in the industry. He also selects the economic profiles for the metropolitan areas within those states, which include localized unemployment rates and job data.

Through the economic development organizations in these metropolitan areas, which Daniel identifies through the state websites, he puts together a list of people to ask about the industry segments with the most unemployed people. He adds the highlights of his conversations with the experts to the profiles he downloaded from the BLS website.

The summary that Daniel hands over contains a list of metropolitan areas, within the five states he investigated, that matched the executive team's workforce criteria. The team will use this list to narrow down its choices to two possible locations.

Sizing the Local Market

Michael, a marketing strategy consultant, recently worked with a client in the printing industry. As part of developing a long-term marketing plan, he and his client are meeting to discuss their target market—advertising and marketing businesses in the metro area. Before the meeting, Michael needs to understand the size of the current market.

Michael calls Liz, a market researcher he knew through one of his professional associations, to see whether she can help locate some numbers. She says she could do some preliminary research to get an idea of what the project would entail. Liz searches the website of the local business weekly and finds no mention of any market studies. She then calls the publisher of a regional business magazine, who tells her he didn't know of any studies that quantified the local market. Liz calls Michael to say that, depending on his time frame and budget, they could take one of three approaches to answering his question:

1. Dig further into the business literature and talk to some local experts to determine whether anyone has already sized the market.

2. Try to estimate the market's size by piecing together any data they could uncover within the decided time frame and budget.

3. Conduct original research by surveying and interviewing businesses within the industry.

Because of the short turnaround time needed for his meeting, Michael selects the second option. After some discussion, he and Liz decide that some very rough numbers would be good enough right now.

Liz turns to the American City Business Journals Book of Lists for the area (www.bizjournals.com/commerce) and totals the revenues for the top 25 advertising and marketing firms. She uses the free features of zapdata (www.zapdata.com) and InfoUSA.com (www.infousa.com) to get counts of companies with the advertising and marketing industry SIC code, which gives her an idea of how many firms operated in the metro area.

When she delivers the results, Liz makes sure to point out these caveats:

- The income in the Book of Lists is self-reported, and not all companies are included in the lists.

- The SIC codes are self-assigned by the companies themselves and are not always accurate.

- This is only a very rough estimate, and in no way does it quantify the market.

After discussing these caveats, Michael decides that this information was adequate for his client meeting.

Extra Tips for Local Economics

⇨ Economic conditions can change suddenly. Select tools that let you set up alerts or feeds to help you stay up to date.

⇨ Beware of "series breaks." Changes in methods for defining, classifying, or collecting data from one period to another make it difficult to monitor economic indicators over time.

⇨ Look for themes, patterns, or other information that can be found in the data. Identify trends that provide insights into a local economy's strengths and weaknesses.

⇨ When looking at business demographics, know the types of firms included in the data. Does it include home-based businesses or those with no employees? Check your source's definition of "small business." The U.S. Small Business Administration's Office of Advocacy defines a small business as one having fewer than 500 employees.

LOCAL COMPANIES

In this chapter, you'll learn where to look for hard-to-find information on private companies and more in-depth coverage of public companies, including financials, strategy, products and services, management, contacts, and so forth. Also covered are sources and tips for finding targeted company lists.

First, keep in mind that finding information on privately held companies—that is, companies that do not offer shares to the public—can be challenging. There isn't much that private companies need to disclose beyond their name, address, and officers, so researching them requires detective skills. Publicly held companies are required to file a number of forms with the U.S. Securities and Exchange Commission (SEC), and these forms contain all kinds of valuable information about the company and its competitive environment. Since the vast majority of companies are privately held, the odds are good that you will need to use all your research skills to dig up the information you need.

About Local Companies

Company information is one of the more sought-after pieces of local business and market research. You might be identifying or counting companies or researching specific companies. Sometimes geography is not your focus, yet local-level resources often provide indepth coverage of local companies. Here are some examples of when you would use local sources for company information:

- Compiling company lists for targeted marketing efforts

- Gaining insights into customers, donors, prospects, and suppliers

- Gauging market potential

- Researching the competition

- Carrying out due diligence before entering a partnership

- Identifying the top companies in a particular geographic region

Before You Get Started

Researching local companies generally follows one of two scenarios. In the first, you know the name of the company or companies you're investigating. For example, you might be keeping up with several of your known competitors and want to anticipate their next moves. In the second scenario, you're indentifying companies within a geographic area in order to, for example, create a list of possible targets for your next marketing campaign.

Kinds of Information

You'll find two types of company information: information provided by the company itself and information provided by others. Company-provided information includes 1) what companies want to share and 2) what they are required to share (e.g., regulatory filings).

Information provided by others can take the form of news, opinion, data sets, profiles, interviews, or other content. The amount and quality of what you find on the web depends a lot on whether the company is privately or publicly held. For example, private companies aren't required to disclose financials, and when they do disclose them, the figures aren't audited. As a result, it's difficult to get an accurate picture of private-company financials.

When conducting research into local companies, you might be looking for information by geography, or you can be searching by company name. Geographically based information answers questions such as "How many accounting firms are within these ZIP codes?" and "Which companies have manufacturing facilities within the Durham, North Carolina, Metropolitan Statistical Area?"

Company-based research—when you're searching by company name rather than geography—generally involves one or more of the following types of information:

- Financials

- Products or services

- Pricing

- Management

- Market share

- Marketing or business strategy

- History

- Public opinion

- Rankings

- Legal issues

- Target markets

- Research and development

- Customers
- Vendors or partners
- Mergers and acquisitions
- Investors

Bumps in the Road

Research into local companies presents two major challenges. First, you're generally working with a lot of small, private companies. Unless a company works in a highly regulated industry, it is not required to make information public. Information about private companies is therefore difficult to find, and your sources are more limited than in research into public companies.

Second, when you do find information about privately held companies, you can't always believe what it says. For example, financials for private companies are provided by the companies themselves, and their revenue can be under- or over-reported. Even financials for public companies should be examined closely.

Company-released information is often biased, and annual reports frequently paint a rosy picture. Also, in a competitive environment—and in an age when anyone can publish or edit content on the web—false information is sometimes posted by the companies themselves or by their competitors.

Decision Points

How, then, do you find quality information about local companies? In addition to identifying dependable sources for company information, take a few minutes to think about your strategy.

Know What to Expect

On the local level, you're dealing with small, privately held companies, so it's especially important to manage your or your client's expectations about the amount and reliability of information that you might find. Asking a few relevant questions ahead of time can avoid disappointment with search results:

- Do you need audited financial statements, or will sales estimates suffice?

- Are you looking for a company overview or for detailed, department-level information?

- Are you interested in what customers have to say, or do you need expert analysis?

- Do you understand the drawbacks to private company information?

Chapter 1, Planning the Trip, covers more about managing expectations, including a tip from a research pro, Cynthia Shamel.

Use Your Critical Thinking Skills

Be skeptical of any company-provided information, especially financials and even filings to the SEC. Gather and compare results from several sources, and look at trends over time. Does a 400 percent increase in annual sales compared with the previous year seem likely in light of what you know about the company, the industry, and the competition? Has your targeted public company issued any restatements of its financials? Do other sources contain similar data?

For information that comes from outside the company, consider any bias in the information. Look for any reasons to present the company in either a poor or an improved light. Perhaps the source is connected in some way to the company or its competitors.

Another issue is data quality, and machine or human errors show up in even the most expensive information products. Whether it's intentional or not, watch out for misinformation. Chapter 3, Avoiding Shady Characters, covers how to develop a critical eye for local sources and the information they contain.

What's in a Name?

When you're researching a particular company, make sure you have the correct name, spelling, and form of business (e.g., Inc., Co., LLC, or Ltd.). Consider all possible alternatives, including common misspellings, name changes, or commonly used names for companies, to add to your search. Directories or news articles, for example, might use different forms of the company name; most people know E. I. du Pont de Nemours and Company as simply DuPont, but it may be listed in company directories by its full name.

Also consider whether your target company is a subsidiary or business unit of a larger company. Sometimes the information you need is available only in documents or sources covering the parent company or larger entity.

Piece Together Private Company Information

When researching private companies, no one source will tell you everything you need to know. This is the time to tap into your creativity. Gather what you can about a company from a variety of sources because each will provide a small piece of the puzzle. Also, make sure you use a mix of company-provided information and information provided by others so that you get a balanced view.

Sometimes you can estimate a company's annual sales from the known facts. For example, the firm may reveal in one source that its revenues have increased by 20 percent in the past year, and another source might provide figures for the previous year. From this data, you can calculate current figures. Of course, you will have to consider the purpose of the research and how the information is going to be used before deciding if extrapolated figures are adequate. While you might not want to include them in your business plan, they could be useful when you want to get a sense of the competitive environment. Sometimes, it's all you have.

Best Places to Look

Company information can be found in the following types of sources:

- News articles or reports (interviews, articles about— all media types)
- Management biographies
- Analyst reports
- Annual reports
- SEC filings
- Company profiles
- Press releases
- White papers
- Presentations
- Credit reports
- Market research reports

But how do you find company information *and* drill down to the local level? Adding geographic parameters to company research makes any project more challenging, and it limits the number of sources available. The following resources will simplify your search for information about local companies.

Company Directories and Databases

Company directories and databases are merely large lists of businesses, with entries for each company. The depth of the information varies by product, as does the ability to filter and sort by company, sales, number of employees, and geography.

The quality of the data you find in these resources depends on two factors:

- The accuracy of the company-provided information: Have companies under- or overreported their financials? Since the data was published, has the company gone through any major changes, such as a merger or an acquisition?

- What the directory or database provider does with the information: Is the data updated on a regular basis? What quality control measures are in place? To what level of geography can you narrow your search?

Following are some of the more widely used directories and databases that allow for local-level searching, making it easier for you to create targeted company lists or learn about specific companies within a particular geographic region.

zapdata

zapdata (www.zapdata.com) is a fee-based product, but with free registration you can use many of the features of this company directory. The data comes from Dun & Bradstreet and covers more than 80 million businesses, more than 14 million of which are U.S. companies. You can search company records by state, metropolitan statistical area, city, or ZIP code, so zapdata is a great tool for breaking down information by geography, as well as by industry or by company characteristics.

Under the Prospects Lists tab on the zapdata website, customize your search by selecting location, industries, company demographics, job functions, or other specialty data. After clicking View Results, you get a count and can view a list of companies. This makes it easy to see, for example, whether a market is oversaturated or to find top employers within a particular geographic area. Fees for downloading company lists or individual records vary according to the level of detail.

InfoUSA.com

You can also get company counts at InfoUSA.com (www.infousa. com), which is part of the Infogroup suite of products. As of 2010, InfoUSA.com's database included 14 million U.S. businesses. Although InfoUSA sells business mailing lists, it provides counts for free, as zapdata does. What I like about InfoUSA is that it really lets you go to the local level. You can map your geographic location or select metro areas, counties, cities, ZIP codes, neighborhoods, or even mail carrier routes.

ThomasNet

ThomasNet (www.thomasnet.com), another well-known company directory, provides basic information about manufacturers, distributors, service companies, and manufacturers' representatives. With more than 607,000 North American industrial companies organized by 67,000 product and service categories, ThomasNet is very useful for finding out how many and what kind of industrial companies operate in a particular place. You can also use it for identifying vendors.

To find companies that serve or are located in a specific location, enter the state in your search. You can then refine the results by entering values for the number of miles within a particular postal code.

Once you have a company name, you can view the company profile, which contains product information, locations, geographic markets, and key personnel. Also look for news and press releases about the company.

Other Directories

Look for business-to-business suppliers, leads, and other contacts through Kellysearch (www.kellysearch.com), which includes information on 600,000 U.S. suppliers and more than 2 million companies from around the world. Head to the advanced search page, where you can search by company name, industry, keyword, or city or town. Click on the name of any company and view a brief overview with products and services, locations, and contact information. The overview even includes an email form for sending requests to the company.

Several other directories can be used for simple lookups such as address and phone number and are more suited for identifying companies than for uncovering in-depth information about them. Features such as maps and directions can vary, but all have location-based searching:

- AnyWho Yellow Pages (www.anywho.com/yp): Search for businesses by name, location, or distance or browse by state and city.

- DexKnows (www.dexknows.com): More than just an online telephone directory, DexKnows has evolved in recent years with the addition of maps, reviews, images, business overviews, and other social web features.

- Superpages.com (www.superpages.com): Use the advanced search feature to search by distance, address, phone number, city, state, ZIP code, or other geographic unit.

- ZoomInfo (www.zoominfo.com): From the homepage of this people and company directory, click the Companies tab and follow the link for advanced search. It offers a feature for searching by country, state, metro region, or ZIP code. Use caution with this site, however, since the information is gathered from webpages by computer programs rather than compiled by humans, and it's more prone to error than other directories are.

Company Websites

When you're researching a specific company, start with the company's own website. The types, quality, and amount of information you find will vary greatly from company to company, but you can use other sources to fill in any gaps.

The kinds of information you can gather through company websites often include the following:

- Locations and facilities

- Products and services

- Pricing and pricing models

- Employment opportunities

- Partnerships, vendors, and suppliers

- Company history

- Community involvement

- Investor information

- Press releases and transcripts of calls with analysts

- Marketing and business strategy

- Research and development

- Management

Remember that this is purely company-provided information and is sometimes biased. In addition, the information you find on a company website might not be complete. Highly competitive information generally won't be there, and companies sometimes don't post full sets of their press releases, financials, or other documents.

The following tips will help you quickly gather information from a company website:

- Print a copy of the site map, if available, and check off each section as you finish exploring it.

- Use the site's search feature or the Search Within a Site or Domain option on Google's advanced search page.

- Look at past versions of the site at the Internet Archive (www.archive.org), a collection of archived versions of websites dating back to 1996.

- Use specialized software to monitor website changes, including Copernic Tracker (www.copernic.com) and WebSite-Watcher (www.aignes.com).

Another option for learning more about your target company is to go to the websites of suppliers, partners, or other firms doing business with the company. Using Google's advanced search page, see what other sites link to a company website. You'll often uncover information that the company hasn't released on its own. Look at press releases, company announcements, or parts of the website that talk about partnerships, clients, or other relationships.

Adobe Acrobat Pro for
Private Company Research

Amelia Kassel, MarketingBase

A key method for beginning private company research is to fully investigate the company's website. You want to learn as much about what the company says about itself as you can, and then verify information from other sources when applicable. Commonly, exploring a site entails using the site indexes and tabs. When a company includes a site map, it's often faster to look there first in order to pick and choose the links of most interest. However, moving from link to link at a company site can be slow. To enhance productivity, you can download the site for faster scanning of webpages. Adobe Acrobat 9 Pro facilitates this process in six short steps that take a matter of seconds:

1. Launch Adobe Acrobat Pro.

2. Click on Create PDF from Website.

3. Type or paste the URL for the site in a box.

4. Click on Capture Multiple Levels.

5. Click on Get Entire Site.

6. Click on Create.

Once downloaded into a PDF file, the site is available for quick scanning. Links to each page are hot linked within the file, should you want to click through to the site to double-check anything.

Private company websites are generally small compared with those of large corporations, associations, or organizations, but they sometimes can take from one hour to many hours to download. Large or graphics-intensive sites require more time. The speed of your internet connection or computer processing capability may affect how fast a site downloads. The good news is that Adobe Acrobat 9 Pro works in the background, and you can continue using your computer during the download. When the download is complete, save the file and open it. Skim through the pages by paging down or use the Find or Search capabilities in the file for locating keywords important for your research.

U.S. Securities and Exchange Commission Filings

The SEC requires that public companies file and make public their regular reporting forms, which are a great source of company-related information. In addition to financials and other required details on public companies, SEC filings, especially Form 10-K (annual filing), can uncover information about private companies doing business with public companies. Also, some private companies may have at one time considered or are currently considering going public, so they will have filed an S-4 form with the SEC.

Public companies file the required forms through the Electronic Data Gathering, Analysis, and Retrieval (EDGAR) system, which you can search for free at www.sec.gov/edgar.shtml. This works fine for company searches, but when searching geographically, you'll need fee-based sources. For example, you can search EDGAR filings through Morningstar Document Research (document research.morningstar.com), which offers a Geographic Filter section on its advanced search page. More about using Morningstar Document Research and other premium sources can be found in Chapter 9, Paying at the Pump.

Local News

Turn to news sources to augment what you've found in a company directory, profile, or website. It doesn't matter whether they're large or small, private or public, local companies are generally well-covered by the local press. General and business news sources consider their homegrown companies to be newsworthy, and coverage is generally more in-depth and ongoing than what's in national sources. Local news also provides a local viewpoint, something else that can't be found from national news outlets.

In addition to filling in the blanks on a particular company, use local news sources to help you identify target companies. Perhaps you are looking for sponsors or donors, and you'd like to know which local companies support the arts or have organized community-service programs. You might be planning a new marketing campaign, and you want to put together a list of companies that get the most exposure within your geographic markets.

Remember that news comes in all forms, including video and audio. Be sure to check radio and television news, in addition to newspaper websites. As traditional news outlets look for new business models, many are involved in blogging and other social media. Hyperlocal news sources, which focus on the community level, sometimes provide insights into some of the smallest companies within a particular geographic area.

To search the local news for company-related information, you can go to the websites of local news outlets. Another option is a news search engine, which will allow you to search a variety of sources at once while narrowing the search to just local sources. The following tools are especially useful for searching local news for company information. Additional sources can be found in Chapter 2, Packing the Essentials:

- Yahoo! Directory (dir.yahoo.com) and Google Directory (directory.google.com): From the homepage, follow the links for the news section. From there, you can get to a section for news websites by region, where you can browse links by country, state, or other geographic unit. These links will take you to the websites of magazines, newspapers, radio and television sites, and other types of news media. The Google Directory offers the same functionality with slightly different content.

- NewsLink (www.newslink.org): This directory contains links to news sites throughout the world, including newspapers, magazines, television, and radio. Probably the quickest way to drill down to your particular area is to browse by location, so follow the links for state-by-state listings.

- Newspapers.com (www.newspapers.com): As the name implies, this resources covers just newspapers. The advanced search page for U.S. newspapers allows you to search by title, state, city, and frequency.

- Google News (news.google.com) and Yahoo! News (news.yahoo.com): Both these news search engines provide, through the Google News advanced search page and Yahoo! News Local link, ways to limit your search to just the news providers from a specific location. These news search engines will save time since you're searching multiple sources at once.

- American City Business Journals (www.bizjournals.com): From the publisher of weekly business newspapers in 40 metropolitan areas, this site offers free articles with a local view. You can also purchase American Business Journals Book of Lists for more than 60 cities, which includes information about the top companies within those areas. These lists are a valuable source of leads and insights into local industry segments.

Local Organizations

Local organizations are a great resource when you need to fill in the blanks about local companies. Chambers of commerce, economic development organizations (government and nongovernment), and association chapters gather and share information about top regional employers and the largest companies within certain industries.

The following sites will help you identify local organizations so that you can tap into their company-related resources:

- Chamber of Commerce Directory (www.chamberof commerce.com/chambers)

- Economic Development Directory (www.ecodev directory.com)

- Tourism Offices Worldwide Directory (www.towd.com)

- American Society of Association Executives (www.asaecenter.org/Community/Directories/ associationsearch.cfm)

- GuideStar (www2.guidestar.org)

Visit the organization's website and look for sections containing information about local companies, including their membership or business directories. I recommend not limiting your search to the web and urge you to see what else you can find through phone research. A phone call to key people within an organization will often complement what you discover through an organization's website.

Social Media

The social web, including blogs, online discussion lists, Twitter, and social networking sites, is all about conversations—and people talk about companies all the time. In addition, more and more companies are now participating in these conversations. The use of social media is booming on the local level, and with a strategy, some time, and some patience, these tools make a nice addition to your company research. The following sections cover tips for mining location-based company information from the social web.

Social Networking Sites

You can gather company-related information using the social-networking profiles for companies, groups, and people. Following is a description of company searching in two social networking sites, Facebook and LinkedIn.

There's no way to search for companies by location in Facebook (www.facebook.com), so this site works best when you need to find information about or make contacts in a known company. Start from your Facebook homepage (free registration required), and enter a company name into the search box. Facebook then sorts the results by People, Groups, Pages, and other types. Company information can usually be found through Groups or Pages as these profiles are often company-related. Also look at the results for People to identify people who mention your target company in their profiles. Approaching people through Facebook can be tricky, though, since many consider this tool more for personal than for business use. Your access to people and groups is restricted since Facebook users can limit who can view their profile, and you may have to join a group in order to contact members.

LinkedIn (www.linkedin.com), which also requires free registration, is used more for business than Facebook is, so it's easier to approach people for research purposes via LinkedIn. LinkedIn also offers searching by geography. Run a company search directly from your homepage and filter the results by location and other variables. To include location in your initial search, go to the company search page (www.linkedin.com/companies). Also, check LinkedIn Groups for people who have worked or are currently working for your target companies.

Twitter

Twitter (twitter.com) offers a platform for people and companies to post 140-character updates for their followers. These updates provide insights into the latest company developments and into what people have to say about those developments.

In addition to searching keywords and Twitter hashtags (#) through the Twitter main page, you can go to Twitter Search (search.twitter.com) to find companies that are using Twitter, as well as tweets about companies. To add location to your search, follow the link for advanced searching. If you're looking for people who work for a specific company and want to weed out the tweets that merely mention the company, try a tool that searches just Twitter profiles, such as tweepz (tweepz.com) or TweepSearch (tweepsearch.com).

Blogs

Bloggers frequently talk about their experiences with companies and their products. Now the companies themselves are getting into the act, so blog posts and comments are an excellent source for company information. Unfortunately, the current state of location-based blog searching is pretty bleak. Blog search engine Technorati (technorati.com) and Google Blogs Search (blogsearch.google.com) don't provide options for adding geography to searches. These tools work best for researching specific companies rather than for identifying companies.

Also try placeblogs, sometimes called hyperlocal blogs. These cover local-level areas and sometimes mention companies. The searching isn't very precise, and you never know what information will turn up. If you have the time (and patience), however, these localized blogs are sometimes worth the effort for gathering public opinion or inside information about companies. To find placeblogs, go to Placeblogger (www.placeblogger.com).

Discussion Lists and Forums

People frequently air their gripes about companies and products through online discussion groups. Like blogs, these sources are most appropriate when you need information about a targeted company, since tools for searching discussion lists and forums don't offer geographically based searching. One site for searching online discussions is Omgili (www.omgili.com). Through the advanced search page, you can limit your search to keywords that appear in just the discussion title, topic, replies, forum name, and other options, so try using location or company names as keywords. Other discussion search tools include Boardreader (www.boardreader.com) and BoardTracker (www.boardtracker.com).

Maps, Guides, and Other Quick Lookups

Use maps, guides, and other sites for quick lookups when identifying, counting, or gathering basic information about companies within a particular geographic area. These sites generally include a lot of user-generated content, so they're a great way to get residents' views about local businesses. While you won't find in-depth information, quick lookups can make a nice addition to the company information you've pieced together.

Following are some examples of how you can use maps, guides, and other sites of this type for company information:

- To identify companies in a specified geographic region in Google Maps (maps.google.com), start at the main page and enter a business category. Add a ZIP code or place-name to the search box as your keywords. Google Maps comes up with a list of businesses near the specified location, which you can narrow according to distance. Besides pulling basic contact information about each company, you can read customer reviews or go to Street View to see the company's physical location and the surrounding area. To find partners, subsidiaries, and other connections, enter the company name in the search box. Also try this at Bing Maps (www.bing.com/maps).

- At Yelp (www.yelp.com), select a location, and Yelp creates a page with links to businesses in the area. At this page, you can search further by keyword or browse the list of categories, including restaurants, shopping, food, automotive, event planning, education, and real estate. Key features of Yelp are the customer reviews of businesses, the maps, and the ability to browse business categories. Similar sites include Outside.in (www.outside.in) and HelloMetro (www.hellometro.com).

Putting It Into Action

So how do you put these tips and sources into practice? Use the following examples as a guide when you are determining the best approach to your own research. Each example details the why, where, and how of geography-based company research.

Prospecting by Geography

Kendra is a sales manager for a national printing supply firm. Even with shrinking travel budgets and fewer salespeople to meet with prospects and customers, Kendra is unwilling to give up face-to-face meetings, which have always worked well for the company. Instead, she decides that the team would operate more efficiently and cluster their sales calls by location. Based on the company's existing customer base, Kendra selects three cities in which to focus her department's efforts during the next quarter. Her plan is to develop lists of printing companies within a certain radius of the hotels where the salespeople generally stay.

Kendra isn't sure whether map searching at Google, Yahoo!, or Bing will give her the best results. At Bing Maps, she discovers that in order to locate businesses in a particular area, she will have to download special software—something that is prohibited on her company-issued laptop. She then compares the features of Yahoo! Maps (maps.yahoo.com) and Google Maps and finds that with Google she can limit her searches to businesses within a certain distance from a particular location.

In the search box, Kendra enters the ZIP code for the hotel in the first city and includes the term *printers*. By clicking More Options, she maps all the locations within 15 miles of the hotel. She repeats the search for the remaining cities and, for each, prints the maps and the lists of targeted businesses.

Digging Deeper With Local News

Diego, a journalist working out of New York, is researching a story on a company headquartered in San Francisco. As part of gathering background on his topic, he wants to develop a more in-depth picture of the company's strategy. The journalist had already read the articles published in his own newspaper, explored SEC filings, and scanned the company website, but he needs more.

He decides to see what he can find in the newspapers from the city where the company is headquartered. He strikes out at Yahoo!

News, but he has better results from Google News. Through the advanced news search, he searches for articles in sources from just California. The results page includes several articles that discuss the company's expanding geographic market and product line.

Through the links on the left side of the search results, Diego runs the same search in Google Blogs and Google Images. The blogs come from mainstream and alternative news bloggers, and he is able to gather more company information for his story. He also makes note of the authors in case he eventually needed to dig deeper.

Checking Out the Competition

Sam is the new general manager of a new restaurant in the trendy part of town. With lots of competition, he decides that, in addition to the critics in the local magazines and newspapers, he needs to keep an eye on what customers think about his and other locally owned restaurants in the city. He wants to set up a simple, ongoing process that would deliver updates on reviews and comments about his and his competitors' establishments.

Through his membership in the state restaurant association, Sam is able to identify five nearby restaurants with similar menus and customer demographics. In addition to local magazines and newspapers, he selects three sources to monitor opinions of these businesses: Yelp, Twitter, and Google Maps. Sam selects these sources because they offer location-based searching, and he can set up an RSS feed for each restaurant.

Sam starts with Twitter. Through search.twitter.com, he runs a search for each business. Hashtags and the special features on the advanced search page (including location) make it easy to find the right establishments. On the results page, he clicks the Feed For This Query link so that any changes to the page will show up in his RSS reader.

Through the Yelp website, Sam heads to the city page. He then searches for each of the establishments and sets up a feed for the latest reviews.

At maps.google.com, he searches for restaurants by location and follows the links to information about each of the businesses. By clicking More Info, he is able to get to each restaurant's Place Page. In addition to reviews, Sam discovers these pages include a What People Are Saying About section, which pulls out the keywords from the reviews and lists them according to usage. This helps Sam get an understanding of what aspects of dining are important to customers. Through another RSS feed, Sam is notified whenever information is added to the webpage.

Mining Official State Websites for Company Information

➡ Determine what, if any, government agency regulates the industry in which your target company operates to see what information that agency can provide. Visit the state's official website to help you connect with agency resources.

➡ Locate the business filings database, usually through the Secretary of State website. Search these filings to learn the exact date a company was formed, its legal structure, and whether its physical location is different from its mailing address.

➡ Use a state's official website to locate a state's list of approved vendors, usually found through a purchasing office or agency. These lists can be a great source of company contacts, as well as descriptions of a company's lines of business.

LOOKING FOR LOCALS

When conducting people-related research, sometimes you need to search *for* people who match your specified criteria, such as geographic location, job title, or area of expertise. Other times, you're looking for information *about* specific people. And on still other occasions, you might need to find information *from* people, such as when you want to verify something you've found on the web.

This chapter includes an overview of adding location to your searches for people and using local-level sources for information about people. It also covers whom to call for local business information, how to reach them, and tips for getting them to talk with you.

About Looking for Locals

People research is always geography-based. When you want information about people, you can choose to go to national sources, searching by location to narrow or focus results. You can also head to local-level sources for information about people—information not always contained in national sources. There are several situations in which you might turn to local-level information for researching people. To varying degrees, they all involve geography.

In the first situation, you're researching people in a particular geographic location. In these circumstances, the location is as important as the person. For example, a national nonprofit wishing to increase revenue might want to identify and then learn about possible donors in several targeted cities. This example requires two different kinds of research—first, research simply to get names that match your initial criteria and then research to get deep information about each of the people named.

In the second situation, geography-based sources are more your focus than the geographic area itself. In these situations, you go to local sources for information that's more in-depth than what's found in national sources. For example, news and trade publications often feature stories of local business people, experts, or celebrities—people not usually covered in the national press.

In the third case, you're more concerned with what you can learn *from* a person than what you learn *about* them. In local research, the people component is often key. Local people can provide context and opinion and can clear up any discrepancies in your sources. They have a valuable insider's view. In this situation, geography plays an important role since you're using geographically based sources (web *and* people) to find information about a geographic location.

Getting Local People to Talk

Risa Sacks, Risa Sacks Information Services

Local people are often willing to talk and want to be helpful. People at newspapers, libraries, town halls, and local organizations know their territory and who has various pieces of information. But how do you get people to open up and answer your questions?

- Be as open as possible. The more you can truthfully say about who you are and why you want the information, the more locals are likely to talk.

- Do your homework. Every small town and small-town newspaper has a website. Get the names of journalists and quoted experts to contact, and get what they've written or what's been written about them.

- Ask for and use referrals. Locals know each other, and they know who knows what. Always ask, "Who else might know?" and use that person's name when calling the referral. "Mrs. Boynton suggested that I call you. ..." This is one of your strongest tools.

- Listen carefully and match the other person's style. Some people may be fast-paced and want to get right to the point. Others are more laid-back and prefer to be sociable before getting down to business.

- Be appreciative of people's time and their willingness to share what they know.

- Offer something in return. The other person might be interested in a summary of what you've already found, links to a helpful article, a useful contact, or an interesting statistic you've come across. In this way, you both benefit from the conversation.

Before You Get Started

In addition to following a plan and using reliable resources for finding information about local people, it's important to know what to

expect from online sources. This section covers the kinds of information found in publicly available sources, as well as the hazards
involved with using the web for people research.

Leaded, Unleaded, Diesel, or an Electrical Outlet

Just as you have choices in how you fuel your car, you have a number of choices in the kinds of people-related information you can
expect to find through online sources:

- Contacts: basic directory-type information, including
  address, phone, and email address

- Biography: past and current achievements and
  milestones of local people

- Opinion: op-ed pieces by or about local people

- Media mentions: activities of local people, covered in
  articles, video, and podcasts

- Images: video and photos of people (for added
  information and to verify identities)

Most projects require a combination of the various kinds of people information, pieced together from a range of sources. These
sources include directories; specialized search engines; social networking sites; local media; and resources provided by local associations, universities, and research institutes. I cover each of these
sources in detail later in this chapter.

Roadblocks

People-related search is one of the fastest-growing areas of the web.
Thanks to the development of specialized tools, it's becoming easier to find online information about people. The social web, for
example, provides unprecedented opportunities for delving into
people's personal and professional lives.

Unfortunately, in spite of all the new sites and tools for people searching, it's often a challenge to find credible, authoritative information about individuals. Web-based sources frequently contain inaccurate or inconsistent information. Many resources contain information that's been machine-gathered rather than compiled by humans, so it's more prone to error. Free sources about people generally lack much detail. The professional databases used for researching people are expensive and often limit access to private investigators.

If your research involves talking with people, you will need to be well-prepared because you don't often get a chance to re-ask your questions. With search engines or other online resources, you can refine and redo searches. With people, you have to get it right the first time. Your goal is to be well-informed, ask the right questions, and be mindful of other people's time.

Decision Points

Before we get into specific sources of information about local people, the following sections cover the first stage—preparing for the search. Think about what information you need, make sure you're using reliable sources, and if you're talking with people, decide how much information you can share with them.

Quality Is Key

Quality information is crucial to successful business research, especially when you're using the web for people-related research. Reliance on mistaken identities and outdated facts can be costly. Misinformation about people—both intentional *and* unintentional—is quite common on the web.

Take a close look at your sources. What problems can you see that might affect the accuracy of the information? How often, for example, are the profiles updated? Is this information collected by humans or by computers? Does the information make sense in light of what you already know about this person?

That's Confidential

Before you get started on your research, think about any potential confidentiality issues. For example, when you're making phone calls to learn about a competitor, is it OK if word gets back to that company's CEO? Is it wise to let it be known that you're considering several new geographic markets?

Online searching for people-related information also isn't without its risks. Do you want your subjects to know that you've run a search on them? When you go to someone's LinkedIn profile (www.linkedin.com), that person can see that; for example, someone from Company X recently viewed his or her profile (you can adjust your privacy settings to block this). yoName (www.yo name.com), a people search engine, alerts people you search for by email address, although they won't know who is doing the search.

Make sure you consider the ramifications of any intentional or unintentional release of information about you, your business, or your project. Once that information is out there, you can't take it back.

Gather What You Know

When researching people, there's value in every piece of information you come across. Even if it doesn't relate to your original question, keep what you find and refer back to it. Following are some of the ways to use the pieces of information you gather about local people:

- Use it to verify that you have the right person. This is especially important when you are working with common names. Make sure you have the correct name, including spelling, nicknames, or other variations. Compare the information in your sources to any known facts about the person.

- Use it to lead you to new sources. Is the person you're researching a member of any association? Organizations sometimes publish information about members in newsletters or other publications. Use creativity when looking for leads.

- Use it to check for accuracy in your sources. Does the person's educational history match what's in other sources? Is this really the individual's current place of employment, or did you read elsewhere that he or she has moved on?

Best Places to Look

People information can be found in several online sources. Where you go for information depends on whether you are searching for people or looking for information about a known person. It also depends on the questions you're asking. This section covers key resources and tips for extracting their local-level information.

Online White Pages

Like their print counterparts, online white pages directories can be used to find basic contact information, including address, phone number, and email. These sites will also display links to fee-based sources, including credit reports and public records. White pages make a good starting point for gathering information about a particular person, and they always offer options for searching by location.

Superpages.com (www.superpages.com) is just one example of a white pages site. Under the People tab, you can get to contact information, a list of neighbors and members of the household, maps, and a reverse lookup. Also try the business search to find the people behind the listed companies.

Other online telephone directories include 411Locate.com (www.411Locate.com) and Yahoo! People (people.yahoo.com).

Search Tools for Finding People

Once you've found some basic contact information, it's time to dig deeper. Instead of turning to a general purpose search engine, try a search tool that's specifically designed for finding information about people. These tools help you avoid sifting through results that aren't people-related. For example, a search for my name in Google brings in lots of results for Mount Marcy and Phelps Mountain in New York's Adirondack region.

Also, specialized tools for people searching generally provide information from sources not covered by Google and other general search engines, such as databases and social networking profiles. They also include features specifically designed for finding people, including the ability to search by email, phone number, or username.

Here are some specialized people search engines and the kinds of information they provide:

- Pipl (pipl.com) lets you search by name, email, username, or phone number. You can also add a city, state, or country to your query. Results cover a wide range of sources, including personal webpages, blog posts, social networking profiles, documents, and images.

- Wink (wink.com) provides several options for limiting your search using location/distance, interests, schools, groups, career, and tags (descriptive keywords). It's especially useful for exploring people's social-networking connections.

- ZoomInfo (www.zoominfo.com) is useful for identifying people, as well as learning about them. Through its advanced search page, you can search by name, industry, company name and size, and geographic unit (state, metro region, county, ZIP code, and distance).

- Whozat (whozat.com) results include web mentions, social and professional networking sites, images, videos, and Wikipedia (www.wikipedia.org) references. Whozat offers several tools for refining your results, including limiting by location.

Keep in mind that these search tools pull information from web sources using computers, and they tend to be more prone to error than do human-gathered sources. Always verify what you find on these sites.

Social Networking Sites

Profiles and postings on social networking sites reveal a lot about people and often contain information, such as hobbies and interests, not found elsewhere. In addition, social networking sites are a great way to find people who have the information you need. If you participate in these services, you can tap into your own network for local-level business research.

Several search tools, including Google and OneRiot (www.one riot.com), bring in results from social networking sites. For more focused people searching, however, consider heading right to the source. With a free account, you can directly search LinkedIn, Twitter (twitter.com), and Facebook (www.facebook.com) to find, gather information about, and connect with local people.

LinkedIn

At LinkedIn, you can search for a particular person or for people who match your criteria. In addition to profiles, you can search LinkedIn groups to find like-minded people, as well as the Questions and Answers section for subject experts.

The advanced search page lets you limit your search by distance from a particular postal code. Add keywords, and you'll be able to drill down to a particular company, area of specialty, job title, and so forth. Full profiles can be viewed if the person is in your professional network or if you have a premium-level account. If not, you are taken to the individual's public profile, which isn't as detailed. In addition, depending on your membership level, you can send messages to people through LinkedIn, whether or not you are connected.

Twitter

Location-based searching of Twitter requires a few specialized search tools and a lot of patience. Through the Twitter homepage, you can search by a person's name, but there's no way to search by geographic area.

For location-based searching, head to Twitter's search page (search.twitter.com) and click Advanced Search. Here you can find local tweets based on hashtag (e.g., *#Seattle*) or distance from a particular place. Advanced searching also lets you find tweets from, to, or about a named person.

Other, specialized sites offer location-based Twitter searching as well. Nearby Tweets (www.nearbytweets.com) and ChirpCity (chirp city.com) are two examples of tools for finding tweets from or about a specific place.

Facebook

No longer just for staying connected with family and friends, Facebook is now used extensively by business professionals. Even businesses themselves maintain Facebook fan pages, giving researchers more options for finding people within companies. Using Facebook for finding local people and information about them presents a few challenges, however.

First, location-based searching in Facebook is far from precise. To find people by location, enter a name or other keyword in the basic search box on your profile page. You can then narrow your search by city or region, school, or workplace. You can't filter the fan pages, groups, or events by location, so you'll need to play around with place-names as keywords.

The second obstacle is that, through their Facebook privacy settings, many people choose to hide their profiles and updates from the general public, making them available to friends only. Joining a group sometimes provides inroads into people's connections, and maintaining a large network of your own friends can be an asset. In general, Facebook works best when used for clues or leads rather than exact answers.

Local Media

Always incorporate local media such as news, magazines, and blogs into your search for information about people. Stories and opinion pieces about local celebrities and hometown heroes often cover information not included in national news sources. The local business weekly, for example, often talks about the management teams of small, private companies in much more detail than you would get from the *Wall Street Journal.*

If you're looking for someone who knows about a place, find out who is talking about it in the local media. For example, the writers for the *Vail Daily,* located in the ski town of Vail, Colorado, are likely sources for information about the future of the area's ski industry. The following sections include starting points for researching the local media.

Local News

To gather news from local newspapers, television, or radio, you can turn to a news directory or aggregator that lets you search or browse by location. Another option is to go directly to the websites of individual news outlets in your target location and search for names of people. These sites don't usually have advanced searching, but it's worth a try when you're focusing on one location rather than several.

Try these key resources for researching local people in the news:

- Google News (news.google.com) includes advanced searching by location or by author.

- Topix (www.topix.com) collects news from various sources and organizes the items it finds by location.

- American City Business Journals (www.bizjournals. com) publishes weekly business newspapers in 40 cities.

- NewsVoyager (www.newsvoyager.com) will take you to the websites of daily, weekly, and college newspapers.

- TV Station Web Page Directory (www.tvweb directory.com) lists links to the websites of television stations throughout the world.

- Radio-Locator (www.radio-locator.com) includes U.S. and non-U.S. private and public radio station webpages and audio streams.

Chapter 2, Packing the Essentials, includes additional sites for finding local-level news sources and articles.

Local Magazines

You can also turn to regionally focused magazines to find local experts and learn more about local people. Go beyond the business-

and news-related magazines, and you'll come across an authority on just about any topic. For example, the food critic for *5280,* a Denver-based magazine for general audiences, would be a good source for up-to-date information about executive chefs working in the city.

An easy way to identify magazines by location is through the Google Directory (directory.google.com) or the Yahoo! Directory (dir.yahoo.com). In the news section of both sites, follow the link for magazines, and you'll see a heading for regional publications.

Local Blogs

Location-based blogs, also known as hyperlocal blogs, provide an insider's view of a geographic area. The quality of the content varies greatly, and searching—especially by location—is by no means exact. Local blogs, however, are extremely useful for researching local people.

In addition to focusing on location, local blogs cover virtually every topic. It's easy to identify experts, including authors, people they're writing about, and people who post blog comments. On the other hand, if you're researching specific people, results are often hit-and-miss.

To find hyperlocal blogs, try using your location and/or targeted person's name as keywords in general blog search tools such as Technorati (technorati.com) or Google Blogs Search (blog search.google.com). You can also try these specialized sites to search for blogs, people, and places:

- Placeblogger (www.placeblogger.com), a directory of location-related blogs from all over the world, lets you search by place-name.

- InOtherNews.us (www.inothernews.us) organizes U.S.-based news blogs by state. Through this site, you can find journalists from nontraditional media outlets.

- Best of the Web Blog Directory (blogs.botw.org) includes a Regional category, with blogs listed by state. Another directory that lets you browse blogs by location is Globe of Blogs (www.globeofblogs.com).

Local Organizations

Tap into the expertise of the people behind local organizations, or use resources from organizations for finding information about local people. Try local chapters of national associations, in addition to chambers of commerce, special interest groups, and nonprofits.

Many organizations post their membership directories in the public areas of their websites, which can help you identify local people. Also check for prominent people within these organizations, such as board members or staff. Take a look at the people writing articles in the groups' newsletters or other publications.

When you're researching a particular person, identify any group affiliations. Head to the websites of these organizations to mine what information is available there. Has this person written any articles for or been spotlighted in an organization's publication? Does the person's listing in the organization's membership directory provide any additional insights?

Use directories that let you find organizations by geography. The American Society of Association Executives website (www.asae center.org) offers a directory of associations that's searchable by topic and location. From the homepage, click Community and then follow the link for Gateway to Associations (www.asaecenter.org/Community/Directories/associationsearch.cfm). Another source, GuideStar (www2.guidestar.org), includes nonprofit organizations and provides location-based searching. Through this site, you can view the latest tax reporting forms for nonprofits with more than $25,000 per year in revenues. These documents contain information about the key people within the organizations.

College and University Websites

Academic institutions are a great source of people with local and subject expertise. College and university websites help you identify experts, and—by researching their writings and credentials—you can evaluate their expertise. In addition, you can ask knowledgeable people within these institutions to direct you to local sources.

A great tool for quickly identifying all the colleges and universities in a particular area is Peterson's (www.petersons.com). Its advanced searching lets you search by location, and there's an option for limiting your search to just graduate schools. School profiles vary greatly, but in addition to a link to the school's website, you'll generally get a brief overview and information about majors and degrees, faculty, and contacts. Another compilation of links to university websites is called simply U.S. Universities, from the University of Texas at Austin (www.utexas.edu/world/univ/state).

Once you reach the college or university website, visit the following sections or pages of the site to identify possible experts or people who can refer you to the experts:

- Departments: Is this institution known for a particular department? If so, who is in charge, and who are the faculty members?

- Professors: Check their personal webpages for articles, presentations, curriculum vitae, and so forth.

- Libraries: Look for librarians who are subject specialists and for topical web guides on the library website (usually in an area that covers research help).

- Alumni associations: Search directories for people within a particular company or industry. Talk to the people who run the alumni department to see whether they can provide any leads.

- Affiliated research institutes: Is there a specialized
  university-supported organization that covers, for
  example, the regional business climate?

Putting It Into Action

Whether you're identifying local people or trying to learn more
about them, you need to take a cautious approach to people searching. The following examples illustrate how to use multiple, reliable
sources to piece together information about local people.

Recruiting People

Chris, a recruiter, is asked by a large national company to identify
possible candidates in a particular city to take a leading role as the
head of community affairs. The company's goal is to develop a positive presence in the community, and it wants to make sure the person they recruit is both highly visible and well-respected in the
community.

Chris' plan is to scan news articles and other sources to generate a
list of possible candidates. He decides that these sources will help
him find who was winning awards, receiving honors at local events,
or serving on boards or who seemed to have a high profile in the city.

At the ABYZ News Links site (www.abyznewslinks.com), Chris
links to the websites of the major daily newspaper in the targeted
city. After scanning the columns and articles that covered the local
social scene and business honors, Chris makes note of a few names,
but he soon realizes he needs a more focused approach.

Through GuideStar, Chris identifies the largest foundations in the
city and lists the names of the board members. At the chamber of
commerce website, he links to the policy-related committees and
adds the chairs of those committees to his list. He returns to the
newspaper's website and uses its search engine to run a search for

each name on his list. He opens a spreadsheet and enters the number and type of mentions for each person.

Based on the spreadsheet data and the information in the news articles, Chris is able to narrow his list to 10 possible candidates. Through LinkedIn, Yahoo! People (people.yahoo.com), and the chamber of commerce member directory, he finds contact information for these people. After conversations with some of those on his list, Chris forwards to his clients the names of two highly qualified and interested candidates.

Finding the Experts

As part of an economic development project, Dolores is tasked with identifying experts in technology transfer from several metropolitan areas across the U.S. She is short on time, so she decides to first focus on university-based experts.

Using Google Maps (maps.google.com) and pairing location names with the keyword *universities*, Dolores finds universities within each metropolitan area. For each institution she runs a search in Google, entering the full name with the phrase "*technology transfer.*" She is then able to link to university-based technology transfer offices for each location. At these sites, she finds names and contact information from lists of committees, administrators, and so forth.

Dolores' next step is to evaluate the experts. She goes to the professors' websites and scans their curriculum vitae, publications, research projects, and other documents. In this way, Dolores is able to see who was most active in technology transfer and in what technologies they specialized. Before contacting any of the experts, she pulls some additional background on each through LinkedIn and Pipl. The information she finds through these sites helps her fill in the information gaps and "warm up" her calls.

Creating a Donor Profile

Ellen works for a national nonprofit organization. As part of its strategic planning for an upcoming donor drive, her team is compiling profiles of potential donors. Ellen is tasked with the first phase of the project, using the free web to gather as many details as possible for her profile template and prepare for additional searching in fee-based sources. In searching the free web, Ellen plans to spend no more than 30 minutes per prospect.

For these types of projects, Ellen generally uses the following sources:

- Two telephone directory–style websites, DexKnows (www.dexknows.com) and Superpages.com (www.superpages.com)

- Two people-search sites, Pipl and ZoomInfo

- Two general-purpose search engines, Google and iSEEK (www.iseek.com)

The two directory-style websites, DexKnows and Superpages. com, help Ellen verify names, including spelling, nicknames, and any variations, such as a middle initial. She also makes note of the contact information. Both Pipl and ZoomInfo allow for searching by location, and Ellen gathers what she can about employment, affiliations, and memberships, comparing the results from these two sources. Through these people-search tools, Ellen finds her subjects' LinkedIn and other social networking profiles. In Google, she enters each person's name and home state into her search, and at iSEEK, she searches by name and filters the results by place through links on the search results page. These search engines lead her to additional details contained in documents such as press releases and presentation slides. Finally, she makes note of the subjects listed on the Topics folders, which will be used to build searches in the project's second phase, using fee-based sources to fill in profile details.

Bonus Tips for Researching Local People

⇨ When you need information from people, pick up the phone rather than sending an email. Between spam filters and over-filled inboxes, it's hard for people to tell whether they've read your message or have any interest in helping you out.

⇨ Know what's ethical and legal. It's never OK to misrepresent yourself when calling someone for research. Make sure you respect the confidentiality of these conversations.

⇨ Don't forget about using blogs from news outlets. They often provide information about local people and leads to additional sources. Check newspaper, television, and radio websites for a blog section, and see who's writing about what and whom.

LOCAL ISSUES

Understanding what issues matter to the people living in a local area and learning more about these issues can provide business insights that go beyond numbers, directories, or economic profiles. This chapter covers what you need to know to research the politics, concerns, top news stories, and quality of life in a particular geographic area.

About Local Issues

Local business and market research often calls for digging into politics, major events, regulatory issues, business climate, public opinion, and other topics for specific geographic areas. For example, when a company takes a close look at the top three cities vying for its new headquarters location, it most likely will research crime rates, school quality, cultural viability, and other issues related to quality of life in hopes of retaining as many employees as possible after the move. The company would also need to know about any political issues that might affect the regulatory environment.

Local issues reveal a community's needs and wants. If you're marketing to or starting a new business in a particular geographic entity, you can gain insights into your customers by familiarizing yourself with the community's current topics of concern. For example, are there any pending legislative actions that might require you to change business plans or operations? What are residents' attitudes about urban development in their neighborhoods?

Local issues have an effect on local economies, so they must be considered when you're doing any kind of economic research. They also help put numbers in context. For example, rather than looking just at business demographics, find out the local issues that might affect business performance during the next few years.

Research into local issues is quite complex because it involves a number of aspects, including:

- Politics

- Health

- Education

- Business

- Arts

- Resource use

- Governments

- Employment

- Safety and security

- Environment

- Budget and finances

- Regulatory environment

- Recent natural disasters

- Immigration

- Diversity

- Poverty

Time plays an important role in local-issues research. While the topics generally stay the same, the resources—and the information they contain—frequently change. Current news is no longer good enough. Now we have breaking news and need sources that tell us what's going on in real time. Equally important, what happened in the past can have an effect on what happens today. Understanding the issues related to a certain geographic area, therefore, often requires gaining both a current and a historical perspective.

Before You Get Started

With so many topics to cover, how do you go about effectively researching local issues? The first step is to get an idea of the kinds of information sources that will help you with these projects and some of the roadblocks you might encounter on the path to quality business-related information.

Where to Look

Researching local issues requires a broad approach since it involves many overlapping and time-sensitive topics. It's also important to make sure you have a complete picture of the issues and that you aren't missing any critical pieces. This is one of those areas in which "you don't know what you don't know." Rely on sources that help you quickly gather and put together all the pieces of information about the issues related to life within a particular geographic entity.

These are the types of information sources that are most useful when your research is related to local issues:

- Media coverage: From all types of outlets and in all kinds of formats, look for articles and stories that cover your topic over time.

- Surveys and opinion polls: The government, local organizations, and the media frequently conduct and report on feedback from residents and businesses.

- Interviews: One-on-one conversations help gather what you can't find through surveys or online searching. You can either conduct your own interviews or read accounts of interviews done by others.

- Issue-related collections: Libraries, local groups, government agencies, and other organizations often create web-based collections of links, documents, and other resources focusing on topics related to their geographic area.

- Statistics: Demographics and economic data produced by the government and local associations help quantify many local issues.

- Real-time information: Specialized web tools help you mine social media and breaking news to learn what's going on and what people are saying right now.

Watch Out

Researching local issues requires some caution and the time to take a few extra steps. When talking about politics, government, or other hot topics, opinions—rather than just data and other facts—come into play. It's sometimes difficult to separate the opinion of the majority of a group from that of a smaller, more vocal subset of the group. This is an area in which it really pays to use a wide variety of sources *and* seek out all sides of a discussion.

Remember that local issues don't exist in a vacuum. Answers to questions about local politics or regulatory issues, for example, are affected and sometimes determined by what's happening on the state and national level. Cities within large metropolitan areas often work cooperatively to solve regional problems. Therefore, research into what's important to the people and businesses in a small geographic area requires an awareness of sources and information for larger or related geographic areas.

Decision Points

With so many topics, opinions, and sources, you'll need to take a strategic approach to researching local issues. The following sections include tips for learning about topics that matter to people and businesses in a particular geographic area.

Focus on Local

When researching issues on the local level, it's a good idea to get as close to the source as possible. To get a true picture of the local landscape, use information resources that focus on or are from your targeted location. Also, you'll make better use of your time by turning to resources that concentrate on local information because coverage will be broader and deeper than in sources that aren't locally focused.

There's no better source for the local angle than the locals themselves. As you search the web, make note of the people listed on the sites you visit. Who are writing the stories, running the government agencies, compiling the statistics? These are the experts to call when the information you need is not on the web. They can tell you the stories that don't make the morning paper or the evening newscast. (Chapter 7, Looking for Locals, goes into more depth about locating and learning from the locals.)

Always Ask Why

Local issues create strong opinions. People and organizations try to push their own agendas, and opinions are often based on limited facts or experiences. When doing this type of research, check for biases by asking yourself why someone would publish this information. What might affect someone's account of local issues? Is the information coming straight from its source, or has it been manipulated for the sake of making a point? This step will take a bit of time *and* critical-thinking skills, but it will be well worth the effort in terms of gathering accurate, reliable business information. (Chapter 3, Avoiding Shady Characters, discusses the need for critical thinking in online local research.)

Think About It

What does it mean? That's the question you should be asking throughout the research process. Otherwise, you wind up with just bits of information that have no real use. Researching local issues requires a multifaceted approach, always focusing on what the pieces of information mean and how they are related. Also, in light of what you're finding, consider whether you should make any revisions to your research plan.

Here are just some of the questions to ask when you find information about local issues:

- What could this mean to me or my organization, now *and* in the future?

- What does it mean for customers, prospects, donors, and competitors?

- How does it affect strategic planning?

- How does it connect to information I have already gathered?

- Should I change the direction of my research?

Who Has Jurisdiction for a Political Issue?

Monnie Nilsson, The Denver Post

"All politics is local." —Thomas P. (Tip) O'Neill, Jr., former Speaker of the House, quoting his late father

Researching local politics can be tricky. Politics at this level is unique because it's largely subnational, yet it's subordinate to higher-level governing bodies. This means that federal and state laws regulate many things that take place at the local level. In those instances, researching a political issue usually means gathering information from state and national resources.

However, local governing bodies retain jurisdiction over a broad range of other issues that impact local life and shape the local political landscape, such as economic development, traffic patterns, and zoning.

To effectively research local politics, you must first know who has jurisdiction over the issue you're studying. A zoning-related political issue could be handled at the federal, state, or local level—or by a combination of governmental entities.

So how can you find out which level or levels have jurisdiction over the specific issue you're researching? A governing body's website usually offers insight into an issue's governing process, pinpoints facts and fallacies, and occasionally serves up a list of political players. It's a good place to start.

I recommend going to State and Local Government on the Net (www.statelocalgov.net), a hierarchical directory of links to specific state, regional, county, city, and town governing bodies. Here you can pinpoint local decision-making entities and their structures. You may learn that decision making resides at the national level or outside a formal government entity altogether—perhaps with a nonprofit, economic, or religious organization.

Other research resources include the following:

- Local (city/town/neighborhood) newspapers: They cover local politics with greater range and depth than most major newspapers can.

- State representatives' individual websites: Here you'll often find insight into local issues and concerns. State representatives tend to be responsive to their local constituents' concerns, and they like to advertise that fact.

- City council websites and meeting minutes: Land use, traffic problems, and city budget issues often incubate locally prior to becoming news stories. Most meeting minutes can be obtained online.

- Cyburbia Forums (www.cyburbia.org/forums): These electronic discussions offer a broad perspective on current problems and solutions on a range of local government issues, many in the areas of urban planning, economic development, sustainability, zoning, and budgeting.

- Stateline.org (www.stateline.org): This site compiles state-oriented news stories, links to elected officials, state legislative summaries, and state-by-state summaries about various political issues, many of which originate at the local level.

Best Places to Look

Several key resources will help you learn about local political, regulatory, legal, and other issues that are important to a community. These include local news, government resources, sources from local organizations, hyperlocal sites, the social web, and libraries.

Local News

Local news stories reveal the hot topics within a community. Elections, budget crises, business closings or openings, natural disasters, and other topics will tell you about the concerns of the people who live or work in your target geographic area. What obstacles are they facing, and how have they dealt with them? How might this information change your business planning?

Look for newspaper articles as well as television and radio news stories. Scan for information in all formats, since many news outlets are incorporating multimedia into their websites. Besides news stories, websites of news outlets contain journalists' blogs, commentary, public opinion polls, and other useful content. Don't forget to include public radio and television in your search, because these outlets tend to focus on local issues. Finally, to get a well-rounded view of the issues, be sure to check some alternative news sources.

The following online tools will help you quickly locate local-level news on any topic:

- Yahoo! News (news.yahoo.com) and Google News (news.google.com): Yahoo! News includes a Local link on its main page. From this page, select any U.S. city or ZIP code, and you'll get a nice view of top news headlines and current events for the region. In Google News, go to the advanced search page and enter a location.

- News and Newspapers Online (library.uncg.edu/
  news): This site offers a compilation of links to the
  websites of newspapers and broadcast news outlets.

- MSNBC.com (www.msnbc.msn.com): At the very
  bottom of the main page, locate news by category.
  Follow the link for Local News and click on any
  state to view a list of cities with MSNBC affiliates.
  For each of the affiliates, you can view news from its
  city and nearby cities.

- InOtherNews.us (www.inothernews.us): This site
  includes links to U.S.-based news blogs, organized
  by state.

- Silobreaker (www.silobreaker.com): Enter a city or
  state and search for news from or about that location.
  The network page helps you see connections to
  people, topics, or organizations related to your
  search.

National, State, and Local Organizations

Local chambers of commerce, economic development organizations, and convention and visitors bureaus make it their mission to
promote the business vitality and quality of life in their cities or
towns. At their websites, you'll find information about the business
environment, leading industries and companies, and employment
outlook. You can often get to these sites using a general-purpose
search engine and entering the location name and organization type
(e.g., *CVB* OR *convention and visitors bureau*) as keywords.

Try advocacy and special interest groups as they generally want
to inform people about the issues in their area. The choice of group
depends on your topic, so think about which organizations focus on
that topic. The Sierra Club (www.sierraclub.org), for example,
makes a good source for anything related to the environment, and its

site includes links to local chapters. The League of Women Voters (www.lwv.org) also has local chapters, and the people in these groups are great sources for unbiased information about local political issues.

You can obtain county-level information from the National Association of Counties (www.naco.org) on a wide range of issues. This organization provides statistics, survey results, and publications on a variety of topics, including the environment, energy, land use, housing, public safety, transportation, and more.

For health issues, visit the website of the Association of State and Territorial Health Officials (www.astho.org). There you will find state statistics plus a directory of links to the websites of state health departments, which sometimes offer local-level data. If they don't, the people in these departments can usually point you in the right direction.

To search for other organizations, go to the American Society of Association Executives website (www.asaecenter.org), click Community and then the link for Gateway to Associations (www.asaecenter.org/Community/Directories/associationsearch. cfm), which offers searching by location. You can also identify non-profit organizations through GuideStar (www2.guidestar.org).

Federal, State, and Local Government

In the name of transparency, cutting costs, and streamlining operations, federal, state, and local governments are adding more and more information to their websites. Look to government websites for statistics, regulatory updates, infrastructure developments, and more. Transit maps, lists of local celebrations, and a directory of town services are just some of the granular, issues-related information that can be found through local governments. Check for news updates and lists of people who could help with your research.

In addition to the State and Local Government on the Net directory mentioned earlier, you can use USA.gov's Local Governments page (www.usa.gov/Agencies/Local.shtml) to help you find state, regional, and local governments.

From the federal government, the following resources can be used for help with issues on the local level:

- For *education,* go to the Common Core of Data, a project of the U.S. Department of Education's National Center for Education Statistics (nces.ed.gov/ccd). At this site, you can find data about public schools and districts in the U.S. Create tables for comparing individual states, counties, metropolitan statistical areas, districts, and schools over time.

- For *health,* the U.S. Department of Health and Human Services offers Community Health Status Indicators at www.communityhealth.hhs.gov. These county profiles include data on leading causes of death, relative health importance, vulnerable populations, preventive services, and other indicators.

- To check the performance or priorities of *local governments,* visit Federal, State, & Local Governments (www.census.gov/govs), from the U.S. Census Bureau. You'll find statistics on government employment and payroll, finances, taxes, libraries, and more.

- For *economic indicators,* go to the Bureau of Economic Analysis website (www.bea.gov) and click the Regional tab. This page includes several data sets for comparing local-level employment, income, and gross domestic product statistics.

- For *crime statistics,* try the Uniform Crime Reports from the Federal Bureau of Investigation (www.fbi.gov/ucr/ucr.htm). Data is broken down for regions, states, counties, cities, metropolitan statistical areas, and even individual universities and colleges.

Hyperlocal Sites

Hyperlocal sources provide news and other information about specific small geographic areas. Hyperlocal sites offer community-level coverage of topics that the larger outlets don't have the time, space, or inclination to cover. Without sifting through a lot of information about geographic locations not relevant to your search, you can identify the issues that matter to the people within individual communities.

Hyperlocal sites generally compile local news, online forums, events information, and business listings. Some include neighborhood-focused blogs and articles. Try these hyperlocal sources to learn what people are saying about local issues:

- Outside.in (www.outside.in): Enter an address, neighborhood, or city to get to local news and information, culled from news sites, blogs, and online discussions.

- HelloMetro (www.hellometro.com): Find city guides, organized by state, with news, hyperlocal articles, events, and even local tweets.

- EveryBlock (www.everyblock.com): This site includes neighborhood-level news and discussions for selected U.S. cities.

Specialized Sites

Many specialty sites provide great local-level information. The following are some examples of topic-related sources of quality-of-life data for smaller geographic locations:

- Sperling's Best Places (www.bestplaces.net): Search for a U.S. city, town, or ZIP code, and Sperling's displays data on demographics, cost of living, housing, school spending, unemployment, religion, and more.

- Trulia (www.trulia.com): This real estate site includes an interesting collection of statistics, housing-market trends, and school and community information.

- LocalSchoolDirectory.com (www.localschool directory.com): With data from the U.S. Department of Education and the schools themselves, this site includes public and private schools. It provides both district- and school-level information, including student-teacher ratios, student demographics, and other statistics.

Social Web

Blogs, electronic discussions, social networking sites, and other parts of the social web offer up-to-the-minute insights into local issues. Social websites generally aren't useful for in-depth information about the hot topics in a particular geographic area, and they can be difficult to search. The social web's strengths lie in identifying hot topics and giving you an idea of what some people think about those topics:

- To find hyperlocal blogs throughout the world, go to Placeblogger (www.placeblogger.com). It's a great way to get an insider's view of the politics, lifestyle, and social issues of cities, towns, and neighborhoods.

- For online discussions, try Omgili (www.omgili. com). Although there's no geographic searching, you

can use location names as keywords to find local
news, comments, and links to related forums.

- Real-time search engine OneRiot (www.oneriot.com)
  gathers what people are saying on Twitter, Facebook,
  and other social sites into one convenient place. Like
  Omgili, this resource doesn't offer advanced searching,
  so try using location names in your search.

- For location-based searching in Twitter (twitter.com),
  use Twitter's advanced search feature (search.
  twitter.com). Sites that specialize in searching Twitter
  by geography include Nearby Tweets (www.nearby
  tweets.com) and ChirpCity (chirpcity.com).

- While you won't find much content about local issues
  and they're tricky to search, LinkedIn and Facebook
  groups can lead you to people who care about issues
  in cities or other geographic areas. Find a discussion
  of location-based searching at these social networking
  sites in Chapter 7, Looking for Locals.

Libraries

Public libraries are the "information hub" of a community, and they
are great places to turn when researching what matters to local residents and businesses. Visit the websites of public libraries in your
target locations to find out about any special collections, subject
guides, forums, blogs, or other resources associated with local
issues. For example, the Madison (WI) Public Library's blog, Check
It Out (www.madisonpubliclibrary.org/new), has a category for
community issues, and the Public Library of Charlotte &
Mecklenburg County (VA) publishes a Community Forum Blog
(plcmcforum.wordpress.com).

Expand your search to college and university, regional, state, private, and other specialized libraries. You can get to the websites for

libraries of all types at Libweb (lists.webjunction.org/libweb). This directory covers library websites in 146 countries, and you can search by keyword or browse by location.

Once you get to a library's website, use the site search feature to find resources related to community or local issues. Also look for contact information for the librarians, who are highly skilled at connecting people with resources.

Putting It Into Action

Researching local issues involves tracking a wide range of topics from a variety of sources. The following sections include some examples of research projects requiring information about local issues and how that information was found.

School Quality

A company is moving its headquarters to another part of the state. The team responsible for site selection has narrowed the choices to two small cities that match the company's requirements. Team members are aware that a nice climate, low crime rates, and plenty of high-achieving schools would help the company retain as much of its workforce as possible after the move. Team members decide to research these and other quality-of-life issues, compiling profiles for each of the cities. Anna, a member of the site selection team, tackles the question of school quality.

For this project, Anna limits her focus to three key educational measures: test scores, student-teacher ratios, and graduation rates. She also needs a list of all schools—public and private—in each city. Rather than going to the websites for individual districts, Anna chooses the U.S. Department of Education website (www.education.gov) as a starting point.

From the department's homepage, Anna follows the link for the Research area and discovers that the National Center for Education Statistics is the agency responsible for collecting and analyzing education-related data. She then clicks through to its site (nces.ed.gov) and finds the Common Core of Data. She is able to search by location, identify the associated school district, and pull up a profile for that district. These profiles provide the number of students per full-time teacher for the district and for each school.

After exploring what other data was available through the site, Anna finds that she could also gather numbers on each district's specialized staff, including school librarians. Realizing that this could be used as another key metric, Anna adds this information to her profiles. She then looks for assessment data and finds reports for just the nation, states, and large cities.

Anna heads to the website for the state's Department of Education, where she locates a database with results of the previous year's English and mathematics proficiency tests. These too are available at the district and school level. She also finds district and school graduation and completion rates.

As she proceeds through her search, Anna adds the district-level data on her key metrics to a spreadsheet, which provides a nice side-by-side comparison. This spreadsheet is added, along with the list of schools Anna had gathered, to the quality-of-life profiles.

Public Opinion

An architectural firm is working on a proposal to design a commercial building that will be part of a new transit-oriented project. Getting an idea of area property owners' attitudes about the project would help the firm frame its approach to the design and how it would tailor its presentations to the various stakeholders. One of the firm's partners asks Don, a business researcher, to help the partners find what they need. Because they do not yet have the business and are only at the proposal stage, the budget is small, and Don needs to limit his searching to free sources that won't require too much time to pull information from.

Don's approach involves searching for news stories about the transit project, especially those covering the opinions of people who own businesses and homes in the area. Because he needs to search by location and perhaps by a particular time frame, he decides that the advanced searching at Google News would be the best place to start. He also wants to consult the minutes of any public meetings and monitor any conversations about the project on the social web. As long as he is at the Google website, Don thinks he'll see if its web search will help him with those tasks as well.

At Google News, he limits his search to just news sources from that state. There he finds several articles discussing what appeared to be two major issues for the residents in that area: tax increases and the process involved with the transit district's purchase of private land. He also makes note of the news sources in the area that covered this story, including the neighborhood weekly newspapers.

Through Google's web search, Don finds the city's official website and looks for meeting minutes. He does not see any minutes, but he discovers that some public meetings had been held in the various neighborhoods through which the rail line would run. Noting the dates of the meetings, Don then goes to Google News Archive (news.google.com/archivesearch). Using the advanced search page, he finds several articles that were published in the weeks during which these meetings took place. They provide a nice summary of some of the residents' comments at that time.

To get an overview of current opinion and to see if sentiment about the project had changed, Don searches the web with Google, using the various keywords for the project, plus the name of the city. He clicks Show Options, which displays the different ways to refine a search. Using these tools, Don is able to run the same search for blogs, videos, and Twitter updates.

Using only Google, Don is able to gather the information he needed for his report to his client. Don's report provides the firm's partners with the information they needed to make several key decisions for this phase of the project.

Industry-Related Issues

After several years of thought, Paul, a local entrepreneur, has finally decided to determine whether the time was right to open a medical-marijuana dispensary. The cultivation, distribution, and use of marijuana for medicinal purposes had been legalized in the state about two years earlier. Although this measure was approved by the voters, the dispensary system set up by the state created a proliferation of these establishments in cities and towns, and there was backlash from residents and government officials. New rules implemented by the city council limit the number of dispensaries within the city, and Paul knows that he will have to plead his case before the city council.

Paul's plan of action is to prepare for the hearing and arrive well informed. He first outlines his questions:

- What is the current state of proposed legislative actions for controlling the medical-marijuana industry?

- What do the people of the city and state think about this issue, and what are the objections to neighborhood dispensaries?

- What are the opinions of each of the city council members on the issue?

At the city's website, under the Business Licensing link, Paul finds the medical marijuana dispensary application and a section with details about license requirements and procedures. In the section covering city council activities, he pulls information about the new regulations, including a summary of the city attorney's opinion on the legalities of these changes. Paul also finds the minutes of the meeting during which these regulations were approved and learns that all the city council members had voted yes.

Not sure if the vote reflected the true opinion of council members, Paul heads to the websites for the city's daily newspaper. He discovers that it was difficult to do any advanced searching and that he is also limited in the number of characters he could use in a query. He scans the results of a basic search using the keywords *medical marijuana*. He finds some articles covering concerns about these establishments and their effect on the community, including proximity to schools, day-care providers, and college campuses. Several articles mention cities that were considering bans on marijuana dispensaries, although some experts predicted that the bans would be overturned in court.

For more precise searching, Paul goes to Google News. He wants to see whether he can find any articles on this topic that mention specific members of the city council. He searches *medical marijuana denver city council (name1* OR *name2* OR ...), using the last name of each council member. None of the resulting articles provide insights into the opinions of individual members, and the city council seem to be presenting a united front.

Paul then uses Google News to find more about public opinion. A search of *medical marijuana (opinion* OR *poll)* pulls up a recent Rasmussen poll indicating that nearly half the states' residents support the legalization of marijuana. He also finds that more men than women supported legalization.

Paul's last stop is the official state website because he wants to see whether there is any proposed legislation at the state level that might affect his decision. He follows the State Legislature link and is able to search for bills with the keywords *medical marijuana*. Paul then sets up an alert that will notify him of any changes to the page.

Based on the information he has found, Paul decided to apply for a license to operate a dispensary. To increase his chances of having the application accepted, he selects a site that exceeds the latest zoning requirements, making sure the dispensary was not close to a school or day-care facility. To address concerns he anticipates the community might raise, Paul also decides to limit hours of operation and to impose minimum-age requirements for entry on the premises.

More Tips for Researching Local Issues

⇨ Find sources by asking, Who cares about this issue? Try to identify which political party or candidate, government official or agency, special interest group, or publication makes this subject its concern.

⇨ Use sources that will help you learn all sides of the issues. Turn to a variety of sources from both mainstream and alternative media, including articles, blogs, discussion groups, maps, reviews, and rankings.

⇨ Expand your horizons, and look at the larger picture. Become informed about state and regional issues and how they affect smaller communities. Compare the concerns of citizens in one location to those in similar or nearby cities, towns, and neighborhoods.

⇨ Put your critical thinking skills to work when researching local issues. Always question or evaluate the reasoning, arguments, and purpose behind what you read or hear about local issues.

PAYING AT THE PUMP: FEE-BASED SOURCES FOR LOCAL BUSINESS INFORMATION

Why would anyone pay for online information when there's so much available for free? Previous chapters in this book have focused on free resources, so why dedicate one to just fee-based options? Sometimes—when you can't find what you need on the free web, when you need it fast, or when you need something beyond basic information—it's a good idea to consider paying for premium. For example, if you're going to spend four or five hours looking for something through the free web, when—for a small fee—you can get it in 30 minutes, what's really more cost-effective? For local searchers, fee-based sources are often the fastest route to detailed information for small geographic areas.

Many fee-based information products and services are geared toward research professionals, with specialized content and power searching options. They often include annual-subscription pricing plans that make sense if you're doing a lot of research on a regular basis. If you're not, or if your budget won't cover the higher-priced annual plans, several of these sources offer low-cost options for local research

In this chapter, you'll find out about the types of fee-based resources, what they have to offer, and when you would consider turning to a fee-based source for local business and market information. The chapter also describes some low-cost sources for drilling to the local level and some tips for getting the most out of your investment.

Fee-Based vs. Free Resources

What are the differences between the free sources and the fee-based? What do you get for your money? Essentially, these sources involve a fee because someone has taken basic information and done something to it that adds value. Examples of value-added features include:

- Specialized content

- Searching and downloading content from multiple sources

- Advanced search and filtering options

- Alerts

- Authoritative sources

- Copyright compliance

- Added analysis, opinions

- Preformatted results

There are situations when, no matter what your business topic or geographic location, it makes sense to take advantage of fee-based information sources. The added value provided by these sources is often worth the investment, for these two reasons:

- You'll save time. Real costs of any project include both your time and your expenses. Preformatted reports, tables, and profiles mean less work. When you don't have to visit the websites of individual sources, you save money in the long run. Advanced searching helps you quickly find local sources and content.

- You'll find information that can't be found through free sources. Many reliable, authoritative sources don't make their information available on the web. Hard-to-find data is costly, so premium is often the only route to go.

Paying for Information— When Is It a Good Idea?

Barbara Fullerton, Morningstar Document Research

"On the one hand information wants to be expensive, because it's so valuable. The right information in the right place just changes your life. On the other hand, information wants to be free, because the cost of getting it out is getting lower and lower all the time. So you have these two fighting against each other." —Stewart Brand, founder of The WELL, one of the internet's first virtual communities

Where Mr. Brand foresaw a conflict, I see a complement. There is a great deal of valuable free information on the web, though it can be difficult to obtain, and there is also a great deal of valuable fee-based information. There are times to use free information and times to use "value-added," or fee-based, information to answer research questions. So how do you decide when the time is right to use fee-based information?

That decision depends on the nature of the search and your level of knowledge. For example, if you're just looking for a copy of the federal Clean Air Act, you might know the right government resource for finding the webpage for downloading the document into several readable formats. In this situation you have no need for a fee-based service—provided you know the precise website and how to gain access to the documents. If, however, you're starting from scratch and use a general-purpose search engine to research the phrase *Clean Air Act*, you'll need to sort through more than 6 million results to find which contains the document. In this case, "free" information has a cost—your time.

Also, if you need additional information about how the Clean Air Act pertains to companies building power plants, fee-based services are a good choice. They could help you find expert opinions about the background of the law, what sections of the law are most relevant for companies building power plants, in-depth information on the power plant regulations, and how companies are using these laws.

It's a good idea to turn to fee-based sources when you need to

• Verify the accuracy and validity of information

• Quickly retrieve and analyze data in an organized fashion

- Clarify information with the availability of customer support

- Customize information for fast retrieval

- Repackage the information in a usable format for clients

  Content-rich, value-added information is priceless to any researcher. Sometimes free information fits the bill, and other times fee-based information is required.

Types of Fee-Based Sources

Fee-based sources come in all varieties. Prices can range from thousands of dollars for a yearly subscription to less than $100 for a single report or data file. These sources cover any business topic and generally offer products in your choice of formats.

Several types of premium resources can be used for local business and market information, including:

- Mailing lists: A good mailing list will help you identify or count prospects or competitors. You can create lists for virtually any geographic location, refined by company revenues, number of employees, years in business, consumer demographics, and other options.

- Maps: Displaying demographics, economic indicators, and other types of information on maps adds context and aids analysis. Fee-based resources generally cover geographic units of all sizes, in custom or preformatted maps.

- Data files: Certain information providers will sell just a table or a chart, which is a nice low-cost alternative to full reports. For those times when you're looking for one or two hard-to-find local statistics, check with the fee-based sources to see whether they will sell only what you need. If you don't see it offered on the web, try picking up the phone and asking.

• Packaged reports: Packaged reports combine a number of pieces of information in a convenient, well-formatted, easy-to-read document. These reports often include analysis, tables, charts, and other valuable features. Several providers of market research and demographic reports offer relatively inexpensive local-level information, and the cost of the report often makes up for the time you'd spend searching for several pieces of hard-to-find information. Many providers will break their reports into sections and sell the sections separately.

• Premium databases: Databases are merely collections of documents—articles, news stories, market data, analyst reports, company records, and so forth. Database vendors organize all the documents in their collection and generally add features for fast and precise searching. They also handle the copyright issues so that you can view, download, and share documents without violating the law.

Pricing

When paying for information, you'll encounter several different pricing arrangements:

• Pay as you go, sometimes called *transactional pricing*: Use your credit card to purchase documents as needed.

- Transactional account: Pay per document, but with monthly invoicing.

- Deposit account: Pay a certain amount ahead of time; document costs are deducted from the account.

- Subscription: Annual or monthly commitments for searching, viewing, saving, or sharing documents. Certain plans provide unlimited access, while others allow only a certain number of documents. Some might include one report plus two or three regular updates.

Tips From the Pros

Tips for Renting a Mailing List

Kathy Mills, Factix Research, LLC

Mailing lists can be found through government licensing agencies, membership associations, professional certification boards, and mailing list compilers. Most government licensing agencies consider the data to be a public record, meaning you may use the data as often as you wish. Other sources usually offer a list rental, meaning you will not own the data and are borrowing it for one use, after which you must destroy it. Usually the list owner will require you to sign a contract agreeing to this requirement and will seed the list with decoys to ensure you abide by the contract.

Major compilers of *business lists* include Hoover's (www.hoovers.com), Dun & Bradstreet (www.dnb.com), and InfoUSA.com (www.infousa.com). The lists are compiled through public records and directories and are sometimes phone-verified. Data can be customized by geography, job title, revenue, number of employees, and industry.

Major compilers of *consumer lists* include InfoUSA, Acxiom (www.acxiom.com), Experian (www.experian.com), and Equifax (www.equifax.com). Data is compiled from many sources, including public records, census data, surveys, catalog companies, and other list providers. Data can be customized by geography, demographics, and psychographics.

Another type of business and consumer list is a *response list.* These lists are compiled through warranty cards, surveys, publishers, charities, and catalog companies. Responders self-report their age, income, and other data. Response lists frequently have a higher response rate than compiled lists do, but they have lower quantities and are more expensive.

Lists can be researched by *list brokers*, who are familiar with the quality of the list and the reputation of the list owner. Brokers use a fee-based database such as the Standard Rate Data Service (www.srds.com) or NextMark (www.nextmark.com). You can also research these databases on your own for free through the print version of the Standard Rate Data Service, available at most public libraries, or through the free but limited version of NextMark at www.nextmark.com.

What's the Value of Your Time?

One way to determine whether a fee-based source is worth the investment is to compare its cost with the value of your time. Here's a formula, which I learned from Mary Ellen Bates of Bates Information Services (www.batesinfo.com), for calculating the true value of your time to you and your employer. Keep in mind that this formula calculates the *minimum value* of your time and isn't necessarily the same as your hourly rate:

- Step 1: Multiply your annual salary by 1.3 (for payroll taxes and other employment costs).

- Step 2: Divide by BILLABLE weeks (52 weeks *minus* vacation, sick, or other time away from work).

- Step 3: Divide the result by 40 (number of hours worked in 1 week)

The result is a fairly good approximation of what one hour of your time is worth to you or your employer. For example the next time you find yourself wondering if you should invest in a $150 market report and you've valued an hour of your time at about $50, think how much it would cost for you to gather and format the data—assuming it can even be found on the free web.

Fee-Based Sources for Local Information

Just because a source is premium doesn't mean it's always useful for local-level research. Many fee-based sources focus on global and national information; there's often no easy way to search by geography. Some sources are powerful yet high-priced.

Many professional researchers use robust, fee-based sources such as Dialog (www.dialog.com), Factiva (www.factiva.com), and LexisNexis (www.lexisnexis.com). These resources compile information from many reliable sources, provide advanced searching for drilling to the local level, and in many cases offer specialized local content.

If your situation or your project doesn't require the investment in these premium database products, there are several low-cost options for reliable and hard-to-find local business information. For local business information on a budget, look for sources that include:

- Options to search or filter results by geography

- Low-cost subscription or transactional pricing

- Substantial local content to make it worth the cost

- Easy-to-use options for downloading and sharing content

To save on information costs, try your public library. Most libraries purchase subscriptions to a collection of fee-based sources, which library-card holders can use (for free) through the library website. The types and number of premium sources libraries offer depend on the library and its budget, so visit the website or call a librarian to learn about these resources and the rules for using them. Owners of information businesses can save money by joining the Association of Independent Information Professionals (AIIP; www.aiip.org), which offers members discount pricing on many information products and services.

The following sections of this chapter feature low-cost, fee-based sources for local information. For each, you will find a brief description of the product, the kinds of local information it contains, its pricing, and its advantages over free resources. Please note that products and pricing often change, so be sure to check the websites for the most up-to-date information.

ACCRA Cost of Living Index

Produced by the Council for Community and Economic Research, the ACCRA Cost of Living Index (www.coli.org) is used for city-by-city cost-of-living comparisons. It is a useful source for people or companies that are relocating or trying to understand target geographic markets.

Quarterly index reports with data for all locations, from 1980 to the present, can be purchased individually or by subscription and in print or electronic formats. If you want to compare the economies of two or more locations, another option is to create inexpensive comparison profiles.

What's it for? Researching and comparing after-tax income, as well as costs for housing, groceries, utilities, transportation, and other economic indicators, for U.S. cities.

What's it cost? Transactional pricing; COLI report back issues, $250; COLI report single issues, from $75 to $125 (depending on format); detailed comparisons, $7.95 for first, $4.95 for additional comparisons.

BizMiner

Well-known for its industry analysis reports, BizMiner (www.bizminer.com) currently offers three geographically based products for identifying local industry trends:

- Local Market Research Reports: These detailed industry market research reports cover industry population, failures, market share, and other data in all U.S. states and 250 metro-area markets. Reports break down data for small businesses and startups and are useful for viewing changes over time (three years).

- Competitive Market Analyzer: A customized, narrative, competitive analysis, this report lets you drill down to ZIP code areas. Topics include general business environment, competitive market concentrations, industry market size and market share, and benchmarks.

- Regional Business Profiles: Use this report for hard-to-find industry trend statistics for any county, metro area, or state. It includes three-year data on industry population, distribution, failure rates, growth, and startup activity.

What's it for? Detailed information about the health of local economies and business environment trends over time.

What's it cost? Transactional pricing; less than $100 per report.

Esri

Esri (www.esri.com) offers geographic information system software and services and location-based data. In addition to premium and basic annual subscriptions and day passes, you can purchase individual reports and data.

Through Esri's Business Analyst Online product, you can obtain U.S. business data and learn about demographics, consumer spending, market potential, geographic maps, aerial imagery, and traffic counts. Study locations can be selected by rings around a point on a map; drive times; hand-drawn shapes; or standard geographic units, such as state, county, block group, census tract, or ZIP code.

What's it for? Hard-to-find, detailed information about customers, especially in small geographic areas.

What's it cost? Subscription pricing; day pass, $149.

InfoUSA

One of several mailing list and list service providers, InfoUSA (www.infousa.com) provides lists that help you identify and count buyers and competitors, based on geography. You can get business or name counts for free. For a fee, you have the ability to download lists, with unlimited use for one year.

InfoUSA databases currently cover 210 million U.S. consumers, 14 million U.S. businesses, and 13 million executives and professionals. Lists can be narrowed by geography, company size, industry codes, or basic demographics. You can really go local by selecting area codes, carrier routes, neighborhoods, cities, or a mapped area. InfoUSA also offers specialized lists such as "New Businesses," "Executives and Professionals," and "New Homeowners."

What's it for? Mailing lists to help you communicate with your target market or to identify competitors within a particular geographic region.

What's it cost? Transactional pricing, varying by list size and type.

Moody's Analytics

Moody's Analytics (www.economy.com) provides economic, financial, country, and industry research for strategic planning and other business applications. Through its Research Store (www.economy.com/store), you can purchase individual reports and tables that focus on smaller geographic units.

The easiest way to find the Moody's products with local-level information is through the U.S. Metro Areas link on the home page. This link will take you to products with the following:

- Detailed employment history and forecasts by 2-digit NAICS codes for metro areas and counties

- Cost of doing business for states and metro areas

- Current and expected economic conditions for states and metropolitan areas

- Recent performance tables for states and metro areas

- Cost of living for metro areas

Note that in some cases, the costs are per location, and you need to buy multiple reports to view and compare data for more than one place. Many of these products include regular updates, some on a monthly basis.

You can also find local data through the site's Data Library, a collection of statistical tables available for about $25 each. Most have national data, but some go to the local level. The tables are organized by subject, and you need to open each folder to see whether it includes any local coverage.

What's it for? Tracking down up-to-date statistics and analysis of local-area economics, including current, historical, and forecast data.

What's it cost? Transactional and subscription pricing, with individual reports ranging from $60 to $440.

Morningstar Document Research

Morningstar Document Research (documentresearch.morningstar. com) provides full-text searching of SEC filings. Required for all publicly traded companies, these filings contain information about companies, people, and markets.

Although you can freely search and view filings through the EDGAR database at the U.S. Securities and Exchange Commission website (SEC; www.sec.gov), Morningstar Document Research offers several advanced features for finding location-based information. For example, you may need to identify companies located or incorporated in a particular place and research their management teams. Perhaps you want to learn about a company's activities in or related to certain locations.

One option for searching by geography is the Geographic Filter feature, found on the advanced search page. It searches the document header, which includes the company contact information. You can also use geographic names in the advanced search page's Word Search. Find what companies are doing in or near a location by adding one or more of these keywords to the search:

- Acquisition

- Partnership

- Target market

- Customers

- Expansion

- Joint venture

To focus the search, make sure your terms and place-name appear close to one another by using a technique known as proximity searching. In Morningstar Document Research, you would use, for example, *competitors w/20 austin* to make sure these keywords appear within 20 words of each other.

What's it for? Searching SEC filings for information about companies and company activity, management, and local markets on a regular basis.

What's it cost? Annual subscription pricing; $249 for Basic level, including training and support.

NewsLibrary.com

A database of articles from thousands of U.S. newspapers, NewsLibrary.com (nl.newsbank.com) is searchable by region, state, or a specific newspaper. Searching is free, and you can purchase individual articles. A monthly subscription allows you to view, print, and save up to 25 articles per month.

NewsLibrary.com solves several major difficulties encountered when using free news sources for local business and market information:

- Having to search newspaper websites one at a time

- Being limited to recent articles only

- Trying to drill to the local level using the basic search tools commonly found on the websites of news outlets

What's it for? Quickly searching the current and back issues of U.S. newspapers in a particular region or creating a custom list of news sources for your searches.

What's it cost? Transactional pricing, $2.95 per article; monthly subscription, $19.95 (up to 25 articles per month).

Nielsen Claritas

Nielsen Claritas (www.claritas.com) provides demographic and census data, marketing software, and market segmentation services. For smaller budgets, Claritas sells several affordable products through its MarketPlace site (www.claritas.com/MarketPlace/Default.jsp).

The value of these products lies in the level of detail. You can find business and customer data on just about any topic for just about any geographic area—no matter how small. Claritas products also include those hard-to-find five-year local projections.

Claritas products include reports, tables, and maps. They offer industry-specific reports, so that if you are considering opening a restaurant, for example, you can find an affordable, geography-based report analyzing the market for all restaurant categories. You don't need an account to make MarketPlace purchases, but if you do sign up for a free account, you can be invoiced monthly.

What's it for? Detailed market analysis, business prospect lists, or consumer segmenting for any defined location, including very small or customized geographic units.

What's it cost? Transactional pricing; most reports priced under $150; business list costs dependent on number of companies and other variables.

PolicyMap

PolicyMap (www.policymap.com), a provider of maps and mapping services, offers a vast collection of data that can be saved easily in nicely formatted reports, maps, and tables. It's an excellent source of information about the health of a local economy and a good choice when you need to compare data across geographic locations or view trends over time. What sets PolicyMap apart from other sources is the way it packages the data. Its products are easily customized and downloaded for use in your own reports and presentations or to email to colleagues.

PolicyMap currently offers more than 10,000 indicators related to demographics, real estate, city crime rates, health, schools, housing affordability, employment, energy, and public investments. While you can get some of the data and reporting features with free registration, PolicyMap's strengths are in the subscription-based data sets and features. For example, you can get estimates and projections for housing, transit, schools, and other topics.

What's it for? Analyzing or comparing local economies and via customized, formatted maps, tables, reports, or analytics to add to your presentations and reports.

What's it cost? Free registration for some data sets; $200 monthly (no contract) subscription for all data sets and added reporting functionality.

Tips for Using Fee-Based Sources

➪ Know what you're getting and what you're not getting. View samples and ask how the information was gathered. What period of time is covered, and does the cost include updates? What geographic areas can be explored, and how are results formatted? Talk to company representatives, take advantage of free trials, and ask colleagues for opinions. Become familiar with these sources *before* you're facing a project with a short deadline.

➪ Get to know the rules. For how long are you permitted to view or use the information? Are you paying for one-time use or for access for one day, or one year? Can you download documents just once or any number of times during a particular time frame? What's the refund policy? Can you share reports or passwords with employees or clients? These details should be clearly spelled out on the website. If not, be sure to contact the site's customer support.

⇨ Learn how to use the special features. Get the most out of your investment by learning about billing options, saved searches, customer service and training, advanced searching, and formats. Does the site offer any customization? How do you search by geography or restrict your geographic boundaries?

Appendix A

Resource Roadmap: Key Sources for Local Research

In this appendix, you will find a comprehensive guide to resources mentioned throughout this book. These resources are organized by chapter, with a brief description of the resource as related to that chapter. In this way, each section presents a convenient, topic-based list of the best sources for local, business-related information. The numbers next to source names are included to help you navigate the short subject guides in Appendix B.

Chapter 1: Planning the Trip

1-01 *Demographics: A Guide to Methods and Data Sources for Media, Business, and Government,* by Steve Murdock, Chris Kelley, Jeffrey Jordan, et al. (Paradigm Publishers, 2006): This book includes a description of geographic definitions in demographic sources.

1-02 Google Maps (maps.google.com): Before getting started on a local project, familiarize yourself with the geographic details of your targeted location. Run a search in Google Maps to view boundaries and nearby places.

1-03 ThomasNet (www.thomasnet.com): This database of manufacturing firms and suppliers can be searched by location.

Chapter 2: Packing the Essentials

2-01 ABYZ News Links (www.abyznewslinks.com): This directory is composed mostly of newspaper websites from around the world, but you'll also find some broadcast stations, magazines, and press agencies.

2-02 American City Business Journals (www.bizjournals.com): American City Business Journals publishes business weekly newspapers in more than 40 cities. Go through this website to search and view free articles.

American Community Survey: See Census Bureau: American Community Survey

American FactFinder: See Census Bureau: American FactFinder

2-03 ASAE Gateway to Associations Directory (www.asaecenter. org/Community/Directories/associationsearch.cfm): Find association websites through this directory. Search by topic, geographic location, and geographic scope of the organization.

2-04 BEA (Bureau of Economic Analysis; www.bea.gov): Part of the U.S. Department of Commerce's Economics and Statistics Administration, the BEA produces what it calls economic accounts—collections of statistics about the performance of the economy.

2-05 BEA: Gross Domestic Product (GDP) by State and Metropolitan Area (www.bea.gov/regional): These economic statistics break down data from the late 1990s forward by industry. Download results in tables, charts, or maps.

2-06 BEA: Local Area Personal Income and Employment (www.bea.gov/regional): Current local-area tables include annual estimates for counties, metropolitan areas, and BEA economic areas on such indicators as employment and earnings, personal income, and compensation by industry. Some of the data sets provide statistics dating back to 1969.

2-07 BEA: Regional Economic Accounts (www.bea.gov/ regional): This page is a compilation of links to all BEA local-level economic accounts, available in interactive tables, charts, and maps. The links will take you to data on regions, states, metropolitan areas, BEA-defined economic areas, and counties.

2-08 BEA Regional Fact Sheets (BEARFACTS; www.bea.gov/ regional): These quick fact sheets, with tables, graphs, charts, and bulleted lists, compare an area's personal income and GDP with those of the U.S. as a whole.

BEARFACTS: See BEA Regional Fact Sheets (BEARFACTS)

2-09 Bing News (www.bing.com/news): Try this search engine for local news. Follow the Local link and select your location (city, state, or postal code) before running your search.

2-10 BLS (Bureau of Labor Statistics; www.bls.gov): Visit this federal agency's website to find data on labor economics, including inflation and prices, employment and unemployment, pay and benefits, spending and time use, and productivity.

2-11 BLS: Current Employment Statistics (www.bls.gov/ces): Look for detailed industry data on employment, hours, and earnings of workers on nonfarm payrolls for all 50 states, the District of Columbia, Puerto Rico, the Virgin Islands, and more than 400 metropolitan areas and divisions.

2-12 BLS: Geographic Guide (www.bls.gov/guide/geography): This handy chart displays geographic coverage for each of the BLS data products. It's useful to see which resources cover, for example, county data.

2-13 BLS: Geographic Profile of Employment and Unemployment (www.bls.gov/gps): Look here for data about the employed and unemployed, by selected demographic and economic characteristics. BLS currently breaks down these profiles by regions and divisions, 50 states and the District of Columbia, 50 large metropolitan areas, and 17 central cities.

2-14 BLS: Local Area Unemployment Statistics (www.bls.gov/lau): This program produces monthly and annual employment, unemployment, and labor force data for geographic regions and divisions, states, counties, metropolitan areas, and many cities by place of residence.

2-15 BLS: Overview of BLS Statistics by Geography (www.bls. gov/bls/geography.htm): The BLS lists all its local-level sources on this page. For each resource, the agency provides a link and a brief explanation of topic and geographic coverage.

2-16 BLS: Quarterly Census of Employment and Wages (www.bls.gov/cew): These tables include data for Census regions and divisions, states, counties, metropolitan areas, and many cities by place of employment.

Building Permits: See Census Bureau: Building Permits

CenStats: See Census Bureau: CenStats

2-17 Census Bureau (www.census.gov): This government agency collects and distributes information about people, households, and businesses and industries, and several of its products break down the data into small local areas. Visit this site for information about Census programs and links for viewing results.

2-18 Census Bureau: American FactFinder (factfinder.census.gov): The principle access point for decennial census data, this site also provides results from several surveys with local-level information: American Community Survey, Population Estimates, Economic Census, and County Business Patterns.

2-19 Census Bureau: American Community Survey (factfinder. census.gov): This annual survey of 3 million households gathers a variety of demographics, including age, race, income, commute time, home value, and veteran status. Create geographic comparison tables for congressional districts, counties, school districts, and other local areas.

2-20 Census Bureau: Building Permits (censtats.census.gov): Try this database for monthly construction statistics (by permit-issuing place and by county) on new privately owned residential housing units authorized by building permits. The Building Permits database includes number of buildings, units, and construction cost.

2-21 Census Bureau: CenStats (censtats.census.gov): A portal for Census data, this site includes links to results for County Business Patterns, Building Permits, and USA Counties programs.

2-22 Census Bureau: County and City Data Book (www.census. gov/statab/www/ccdb.html): Estimates and rankings for characteristics of people and businesses in all U.S. states, counties, and cities with populations of 25,000 or more are included in this resource. The data is compiled from several government sources.

2-23 Census Bureau: County Business Patterns (through American FactFinder; factfinder.census.gov): Through the American FactFinder site, you can view County Business Pattern results for counties and metropolitan/micropolitan statistical areas from 2004 forward. Maps and data tables include the number of establishments, first quarter and annual payroll, and employment.

2-24 Census Bureau: County Business Patterns (through CenStats; censtats.census.gov): Through the CensStats portal, you can view employment and earnings down to the ZIP-code level dating back to 1993.

2-25 Census Bureau: Economic Census (factfinder.census.gov): Conducted every five years, this Census product offers profiles of local economies. It includes statistics on business establishments (only those businesses with employees) by industry and geographic location.

2-26 Census Bureau: Nonemployer Statistics (www.census. gov/econ/nonemployer): This annual data series covers businesses without paid employees, a group excluded from most business statistics. In addition to national-level information, it breaks down data to the state, county, and metropolitan/micropolitan statistical area level.

2-27 Census Bureau: Population Estimates (factfinder.census.gov): Based on decennial census data, annual estimates (as of July 1 of the previous year) are released throughout the year in increasing geographic detail. Create customized tables for comparing geographic areas.

2-28 Census Bureau: Small Area Income and Poverty Estimates (SAIPE; www.census.gov/did/www/saipe): Visit this site for annual estimates of income and poverty indicators for all states, counties, and school districts. View data in maps and tables.

2-29 Census Bureau: State and County QuickFacts (quickfacts. census.gov/qfd): These handy profiles include statistics about people, businesses, and geographic locations and can be found by browsing locations, clicking on a map, or selecting the Place Search link. The profiles cover U.S. states, counties, and cities and towns with more than 25,000 people.

2-30 Census Bureau: State and Metropolitan Area Data Book (www.census.gov/compendia/smadb): Compiling more than 1,500 data items from a variety of sources, this resource breaks down data for states, counties, and metropolitan and micropolitan areas. This resource covers a wide range of topics related to people and businesses within a geographic area.

2-31 Census Bureau: USA Counties (censtats.census.gov): With more than 6,000 data items on the county level, USA Counties is updated every two years. Select handy profiles or individual tables.

2-32 Chamber of Commerce Directory (www.chamberofcommerce. com/chambers): Visit this directory to quickly find local chambers of commerce. These organizations are great resources for finding local-level business information.

County and City Data Book: See Census Bureau: County and City Data Book

County Business Patterns: See Census Bureau: County Business Patterns

Current Employment Statistics: See BLS: Current Employment Statistics

2-33 Data.gov (www.data.gov): This federal government portal provides access to data sets generated by the executive branch.

2-34 Data.gov: State/Local/Tribal Data Sites (www.data.gov/state datasites): Through this resource, follow links to state, local, and tribal sites with local-area information.

2-35 Dialog (www.dialog.com): This fee-based professional database provides advanced searching for finding local content in news, market research reports, and other documents.

2-36 Dun & Bradstreet (www.dnb.com): This company compiles information about public and private companies. Information can be found through several sources, and the content varies according to the source.

Economic Census: See Census Bureau: Economic Census

2-37 Economic Development Directory (www.ecodevdirectory. com): Use this to find economic development organizations, which offer many resources for finding business and market data and information about local issues.

2-38 GovScan (govscan.com): Powered by Google, GovScan searches more than 5,000 city, town, county, and state government websites within all 50 states.

Geographic Profile of Employment and Unemployment: See BLS: Geographic Profile of Employment and Unemployment

2-39 EveryBlock (www.everyblock.com): At this site, you can filter news to the neighborhood, quadrant, ward, and ZIP-code level.

2-40 Facebook (www.facebook.com): Search this site for people, groups, and companies and information about them. Search results for people can be filtered by location.

2-41 Feedmap (www.feedmap.net): Find location-based blogs through this directory. Browse the list of worldwide locations or search by city, state, or postal code.

2-42 Flickr (www.flickr.com): To find location-based images, go directly to the advanced search page, enter your location, and search by tags.

2-43 Fwix (fwix.com): Covering cities and regions in the U.S., U.K., Canada, Australia, New Zealand, and Ireland, this site deals with topics related to business, crime, sports, politics, and environment.

2-44 Google Blog Search (blogsearch.google.com): Blogs often contain useful business information and can lead you to local experts. To search by geography, try entering the location name in your keyword search.

2-45 Google Maps (maps.google.com): Enter a geographic location in your keyword search to find user-contributed photos and maps. Also look for Place Pages, which are webpages that compile information about businesses, cities, and points of interest throughout the world.

2-46 Google News (news.google.com): The advanced search page currently allows you to enter a country or U.S. state in the Source Location box to retrieve articles *from* that location. Another option is to enter a city, state, or ZIP code in the Location box, which will retrieve articles *about* a particular location.

Gross Domestic Product (GDP) by State and Metropolitan Area: See BEA: Gross Domestic Product (GDP) by State and Metropolitan Area

2-47 GuideStar (www2.guidestar.org): You can find nonprofit organizations through this directory with its handy location-based searching. This resource includes financial filings for organizations, with details about the group and key personnel.

2-48 HelloMetro (www.hellometro.com): Through this site, you will find hyperlocal articles and news. Read reviews and learn about local businesses and events.

2-49 HomeTownLocator (www.hometownlocator.com): View profiles for cities, towns, neighborhoods, and subdivisions. Tables and maps compile information from a variety of sources.

2-50 Hoover's (www.hoovers.com): This fee-based resource contains information about companies (public and private), people, and industries.

2-51 Idealist.org (www.idealist.org): This website from Action Without Borders provides a summary and links to organizations throughout the world. Advanced searching features help you find relevant organizations by geography.

2-52 InOtherNews.us (www.inothernews.us): Add some nonmainstream news sources to your research mix. This site organizes U.S.-based news blogs by state.

2-53 LexisNexis (www.lexisnexis.com): This premium, fee-based database includes news, market research reports, company profiles, and other sources. Advanced searching capabilities and specialized content help you quickly drill to the local level.

2-54 LinkedIn (www.linkedin.com): LinkedIn, a social networking site for business professionals, is an excellent source of information about people and companies. Search profiles, answers, and group pages for geographically based information.

Local Area Unemployment Statistics: See BLS: Local Area Unemployment Statistics

Local Area Personal Income and Employment: See BEA: Local Area Personal Income and Employment

2-55 LocalSchoolDirectory.com (www.localschooldirectory.com): Find district and school-level information, including student demographics, rankings, class size, and more.

2-56 Localtweeps (www.localtweeps.com): This specialty search tool helps you find Twitter updates by geography. Use this site to find out about local issues, opinions, and resources.

2-57 Meetup.com (www.meetup.com): Through this site, you can link with people virtually and meet in person or online. It's a great way to get to know people and connect with other sources in a particular geographic location.

2-58 Morningstar Document Research (documentresearch.morning star.com): Morningstar Document Research provides subscription-based, full-text searching of SEC filings. The advanced features include geographic searching.

2-59 Nearby Tweets (www.nearbytweets.com): Use this site to search Twitter for tweets by topic and location. Look for local sources, news, and opinions.

2-60 News and Newspapers Online (library.uncg.edu/news): Visit this site for links to newspapers and broadcast news outlets that offer free access to current, general-interest, and full-text news.

2-61 Newser (www.newser.com): This site offers a local news index, covering major metropolitan areas.

2-62 NewsVoyager (www.newsvoyager.com): At this site, you will find links to daily, weekly, and college newspapers throughout the world.

Nonemployer Statistics: See Census Bureau: Nonemployer Statistics

2-63 Outside.in (www.outside.in): This hyperlocal source includes community-level blogs, articles, and other resources. You can search Outside.in by topic and geographic location.

2-64 Pipl (pipl.com): Search this people-finding site by name, email address, username, phone, or location.

2-65 Placeblogger (www.placeblogger.com): This site helps you find hyperlocal blogs by place-name.

2-66 PodcastDirectory.com (www.podcastdirectory.com): Podcasts often provide information that isn't found in text format, and this site offers searching by major city.

Population Estimates: See Census Bureau: Population Estimates

Quarterly Census of Employment and Wages: See BLS: Quarterly Census of Employment and Wages

2-67 Radio-Locator (www.radio-locator.com): This collection of links will take you to the webpages and audio streams of private and public radio stations from the U.S. and around the world.

Regional Economic Accounts: See BEA: Regional Economic Accounts

Small Area Income and Poverty Estimates (SAIPE): See Census Bureau: Small Area Income and Poverty Estimates (SAIPE)

2-68 Securities and Exchange Commission (SEC; www.sec. gov): Visit this site to search SEC filings for company-related information.

2-69 State Agency Databases (wikis.ala.org/godort/index.php/ State_Agency_Databases): This resource links to databases available on state websites, many of which contain county, municipal, and even ZIP-code–level data.

State and County QuickFacts: See Census Bureau: State and County QuickFacts

2-70 State and Local Government on the Net (www.statelocalgov. net): State and local government agencies are an excellent source of local-level business information. Search this directory by location or topic to find links to government agencies on all levels.

State and Metropolitan Area Data Book: See Census Bureau: State and Metropolitan Area Data Book

2-71 StreetAdvisor (www.streetadvisor.com): At this site, online forums are organized by state, and people discuss, ask questions about, and share opinions about places.

2-72 Technorati (technorati.com): This blog search engine offers no geography-based search options. To find local blogs, try using the geographic name as a keyword.

2-73 ThomasNet (www.thomasnet.com): At this site, you will find information about manufacturing and manufacturing supply firms. After searching, you can filter results by geography.

2-74 Topix (www.topix.com): Select a U.S. city, state, or ZIP code, and Topix creates a continually updated page with news, events, and other information.

2-75 Tourism Offices Worldwide Directory (www.towd.com): Try websites of tourist-related groups for information about local areas. Included are chambers of commerce, government tourism offices, convention and visitors bureaus, and other groups.

2-76 Trulia.com (www.trulia.com): With its focus on local real estate listings, Trulia also devotes a section of its site to ZIP-code–level market statistics and trends.

2-77 tweetzi Local (www.tweetzi.com/local): Use this specialized site for searching Twitter updates by location. Find people, local issues-related information, and sources.

2-78 TwellowHood (www.twellow.com/twellowhood): This site's geographically based searching helps you find local information about people and issues within a region.

2-79 Twitter (twitter.com): Twitter updates offer insights into geography-based issues and opinion and can direct you to local sources.

USA Counties: See Census Bureau: USA Counties

2-80 USA.gov: Local Governments (www.usa.gov/Agencies/ Local.shtml): This directory from the U.S. government provides links to local governments, community service centers, and associations. It also includes a section that lists additional sources of local-level information.

2-81 Wink (wink.com): This free people-search engine gathers information from the web. Search by name, location, email, and phone number.

2-82 Yahoo! Finance (www.finance.yahoo.com): Lots of company information in one location, with free but rudimentary SEC search available.

2-83 Yahoo! News: Local (news.yahoo.com/local-news): This is the easiest way to get to Yahoo! News' local content. Select a geographic location, and you're taken to a webpage with the latest news and video for that place.

2-84 Yelp (www.yelp.com): Browse or search for cities and neighborhoods to read reviews of local businesses. You'll find discussion lists in the Talk section of your location's webpage.

2-85 YouTube (www.youtube.com): YouTube's site will help you find information in video format. First enter a basic search, and then narrow results by location.

2-86 YourEconomy.org (www.youreconomy.org): This specialized site offers excellent information about local economies. It's especially useful for information about nonemployer firms, which often aren't covered in other sources.

2-87 zapdata.com (www.zapdata.com): Through the free features of this site, you can find company counts and market overviews by geography and industry.

2-88 ZoomInfo (www.zoominfo.com): This specialized search engine helps you find information about companies and people that's been gathered through other websites.

Chapter 3: Avoiding Shady Characters

3-01 123people.com (www.123people.com): This aggregator pulls together web-based information about people, including images, documents, email, and related websites.

3-02 Biznar (www.biznar.com): A business-related search engine, this site is useful for going straight to the source and verifying information in published articles.

3-03 BNET (www.bnet.com): This site provides business articles, which are useful for verifying information you find on the web and for identifying leads to sources.

3-04 Glassdoor.com (www.glassdoor.com): A tool for job hunters, Glassdoor.com is often used to research corporate culture.

3-05 Google Directory (directory.google.com): Use this resource for getting to the websites of local news outlets. Follow the link for Regional to drill down to the local level.

3-06 Pipl (pipl.com): This source scours the web for information about people.

3-07 *The Skeptical Business Searcher*, by Robert Berkman (Information Today, Inc., 2004): This is one of the most useful books—if not *the* most useful—for learning about evaluating information you find on the web.

3-08 Wikipedia (www.wikipedia.org): Use information from this site as leads to other sources. Articles with footnotes tend to be the most credible. Check the Discussion page for additional information about an article.

3-09 Yahoo! Directory (dir.yahoo.com): This collection of links includes a Regional subject heading, which you can use to drill down to local sources. It comes in handy for pulling original news articles when checking the accuracy of information you find on the web.

3-10 Yahoo! Pipes (pipes.yahoo.com/pipes): Use Yahoo! Pipes to track trusted sources and have relevant articles and news releases delivered to your desktop.

3-11 Yelp (www.yelp.com): A consumer-review site, Yelp is useful for local-level information about events, businesses, and more.

3-12 ZoomInfo (www.zoominfo.com): This aggregation site collects and compiles in one place web-based information about people. Because the information is gathered by machines rather than humans, be sure to check its accuracy.

Chapter 4: Local Demographics

American Community Survey: See Census Bureau: American Community Survey

4-01 Census Bureau (www.census.gov): The Census Bureau is the major government agency responsible for collecting, analyzing, and distributing demographic data. Click the Geography link to learn about Census geographic delineations for demographics.

4-02 Census Bureau: American Community Survey (factfinder.census.gov): This source provides the most current community-level population estimates. About three million households are surveyed each year, and information is collected about age, race, income, commute time to work, home value, veteran status, and other variables.

4-03 Census Bureau: County and City Data Book (www.census.gov/statab/www/ccdb.html): While not as up-to-date as other sources, the County and City Data Book contains detailed local-level statistics. Data is compiled from the Census Bureau and other government agencies for all U.S. states, counties, and cities with a population of 25,000 or more.

4-04 Census Bureau: Metropolitan and Micropolitan Statistical Areas (www.census.gov/population/www/metroareas): Through this section of the Census Bureau's website, you can find lists and maps of current metropolitan and micropolitan areas and their component counties.

4-05 Census Bureau: Population Estimates Program (factfinder.census.gov): This program provides estimated population totals for the previous year for cities and towns, metropolitan areas, counties, and states. For selected Census geographic units, estimates are available by age, sex, and race and ethnicity.

4-06 Census Bureau: Small Area Income and Poverty Estimates (SAIPE; www.census.gov/did/www/saipe): Visit this site for estimates of selected income and poverty statistics that are more current than those from the decennial census. These estimates are broken down for school districts, counties, and states, and tables and maps can be downloaded from the program's site.

4-07 Census Bureau: State and Metropolitan Area Data Book (www.census.gov/compendia/smadb): With more than 1,500 data items for the nation, states, counties, and metropolitan areas, the State and Metropolitan Area Data Book is not as current as other sources, but it's worth a look.

4-08 Census Bureau: Statistical Abstract of the United States (www.census.gov/compendia/statab): This vast collection of demographic information offers a few tables with data for selected metropolitan areas. You'll need to scan the lists of tables in each section to find those that do.

4-09 Census Bureau: USA Counties (censtats.census.gov/usa/usa.shtml): While only going as local as the county level, this resource offers a quick way to search for information about a wide range of topics, including age, agriculture, ancestry, banking, building permits, business patterns, crime, earnings, education, elections, employment, government, and health.

4-10 Claritas MarketPlace (www.claritas.com/MarketPlace/Default.jsp): This fee-based resource provides low-cost demographic products for any customized geographic area. Claritas is a great source for local-level five-year projections.

County and City Data Book: See Census Bureau: County and City Data Book

4-11 Google Maps (maps.google.com): Use this source to understand geographic entities and their boundaries.

4-12 GovEngine.com (www.govengine.com): State and local government websites often provide demographics for their jurisdiction. Find these sites through GovEngine.com.

4-13 GovScan (govscan.com): Use this search engine to find demographics from local governments. Enter your location or locations with the keyword *demographics* to see what departments or offices provide population or housing statistics.

4-14 Historical Census Browser (mapserver.lib.virginia.edu): Visit this site from the University of Virginia Library in order to view demographic data from 1790 through 1960 and examine state and county topics for individual census years or over time.

4-15 Libweb Library Directory (lists.webjunction.org/libweb): State libraries often collect and share free local-level demographics. To find official websites, go to this directory and follow the link for state libraries.

4-16 National Center for Health Statistics (www.cdc.gov/nchs): This site offers mainly national and state-level health demographics, but it does contain some local-level data.

Metropolitan and Micropolitan Statistical Areas: See Census Bureau: Metropolitan and Micropolitan Statistical Areas

4-17 National Center for Veterans Analysis and Statistics (www.va.gov/vetdata): From the U.S. Department of Veterans Affairs (www.va.gov), this resource publishes official estimates and projections of the veteran population and its characteristics. This site offers data for counties and congressional districts as well as the nation and the states.

Population Estimates Program: See Census Bureau: Population Estimates Program

4-18 School District Demographics System (nces.ed.gov/surveys/ sdds): Published by the U.S. Department of Education (www.ed.gov), this resource includes demographics, social characteristics, and economics of children and school districts. You can get quick snapshot reports, create maps, or select tables to compare school-district–level data from the American Community Survey and the latest decennial census.

Small Area Income and Poverty Estimates (SAIPE): See Census Bureau: Small Area Income and Poverty Estimates (SAIPE)

4-19 Social Explorer (www.socialexplorer.com): At this site, use the free mapping and reporting tools to view historical census data from 1790 through the present.

4-20 Social Security Administration (www.socialsecurity.gov/policy): Several resources from this agency contain local-level demographics about program recipients. Click By Subject and follow the link for Geographic Information.

4-21 State and Local Government on the Net (www.statelocal gov.net): Use this directory to quickly find the websites of national, state, and local government offices. These sites are excellent sources for local-level demographic data.

State and Metropolitan Area Data Book: See Census Bureau: State and Metropolitan Area Data Book

Statistical Abstract of the United States: See Census Bureau: Statistical Abstract of the United States

4-22 Statistics of Income (SOI) Internal Revenue Service (www.irs.gov): From the IRS homepage, follow the link for Tax Stats and then click Individual Income Tax. Scroll to the section for Individual Data by Demographic Areas, which includes county-level income data for taxpayers. ZIP-code–level tables are available for a fee.

USA Counties: See Census Bureau: USA Counties

Chapter 5: Local Economics

5-01 American City Business Journals (www.bizjournals.com): Visit this site to get to weekly business newspapers in 40 cities. Articles in these publications often discuss local economic issues. Follow the Book of Lists link for fee-based information about top companies in a particular geographic area.

5-02 ASAE Gateway to Associations Directory (www.asaecenter. org/Community/Directories/associationsearch.cfm): Visit the websites of local organizations to find reports, statistics, and leads to other sources. Find these groups by topic or geographic location.

5-03 Association for University Business and Economic Research (www.auber.org): Universities and other institutions often contain economy-related departments, research groups, or projects. At this site, you can search for member organizations by state.

5-04 BEA (Bureau of Economic Analysis; www.bea.gov): The BEA provides collections of regional economic statistics not found through other agencies. From its homepage, click the Regional tab to get to statistics on state and metropolitan GDP and personal income and employment.

Beige Book: See FRB: The Beige Book

5-05 BLS (Bureau of Labor Statistics; www.bls.gov): This agency is responsible for collecting, processing, analyzing, and publishing statistics covering labor force status, job and wage data by place of work, and prices and living conditions. For local information, follow the Geography link from the BLS homepage.

5-06 BLS: Consumer Expenditure Survey (CE; www.bls.gov/cex): Collected by the Census Bureau for the BLS, the CE provides information on the buying habits of U.S. consumers. Click the Geography link to find national, regional, state, and metropolitan-area tables.

5-07 BLS: Economy at a Glance (www.bls.gov/eag): These handy tables provide state and metropolitan-area economic profiles, which offer monthly data on the labor force. Follow the Back Data link for historical numbers.

5-08 BLS: Employment Projections (www.bls.gov/data): At this page, follow the Employment Projections link to view 10-year national employment and occupational projections.

5-09 BLS: Geographic Profile of Employment and Unemployment (www.bls.gov/gps): This resource provides annual data on the labor force for states and substate areas. It covers selected metropolitan areas, metropolitan divisions, and cities, with sections for historical and current data.

5-10 BLS: Local Area Unemployment Statistics (LAUS; www.bls.gov/lau): A federal-state cooperative endeavor, the LAUS program produces monthly and annual employment, unemployment, and labor force data. Geographically, this program breaks down the data for census regions and divisions, states, counties, metropolitan areas, and many cities.

5-11 BLS: Mass Layoff Statistics (www.bls.gov/data): Under the employment section of this webpage, you can link to state-level data covering layoff demographics, reasons, and other useful information about the economic health of a geographic region.

5-12 BLS: Occupational Employment Statistics (OES; www.bls. gov/OES): With data available for the nation, states, and metropolitan and nonmetropolitan areas, the OES website provides employment and wage estimates for more than 800 occupations.

Building Permits: See Census Bureau: Building Permits

5-13 Census Bureau (www.census.gov): Probably more than any other government agency, the Census Bureau measures patterns of American lives and business at every level of geography. Follow the Business link and go to the Data by Geography tab, where you'll find a table that compares dates and geographic coverage for the available data sets.

5-14 Census Bureau: Building Permits (censtats.census.gov/bldg/ bldginfo.shtml): A survey of local building permit officials, this site includes statistics on residential and nonresidential construction. You can also get to Building Permits data through American FactFinder (factfinder.census.gov).

5-15 Census Bureau: Community Economic Development HotReport (lehd.did.census.gov/led/datatools/hotreport.html):

Part of the Local Employment Dynamics Program, this resource provides current state, regional, or county indicators covering demographics, economics, housing, transportation, and community assets.

5-16 Census Bureau: County Business Patterns (www.census. gov/econ/cbp): Use this source for county, metro, and ZIP code data. These statistics cover establishments by employment and size of the establishment. ZIP code and pre-2004 data are available only through this website.

5-17 Census Bureau: Federal, State, & Local Governments (www.census.gov/govs): Visit this site for statistics from a variety of programs covering government employment, revenues, expenditures, and more. You can also find results of special-topic surveys (e.g., libraries, criminal justice, and education) and lists of local governments, their structure, and contact information.

5-18 Census Bureau: Local Employment Dynamics (LED; lehd.did.census.gov/led/led/led.html): This program develops and distributes detailed reports on local-level labor market conditions. LED integrates existing data with specialized reporting tools that make it easy to identify historic, geographic, and industry trends.

5-19 Census Bureau: USA Counties (censtats.census.gov/usa/ usa.shtml): Through this site, you can find national, state, and county data from the Census Bureau and several other agencies. It includes economy-related statistics on topics such as banking, business patterns, education, employment, health, manufacturers, and much more.

5-20 Census of Agriculture (www.agcensus.usda.gov): This resource from the U.S. Department of Agriculture is the only source of uniform, comprehensive agricultural data for every U.S. state and county. Tables report results covering all areas of farming and ranching operations, including production expenses, market value of products, and operator characteristics.

5-21 Chamber of Commerce Directory (www.chamberofcommerce. com/chambers): Chambers of commerce often collect and share data about companies, industry, employment and unemployment, and other economic information. This directory of links will take you to these local organizations.

Claritas: See Nielsen Claritas

5-22 Common Core of Data (nces.ed.gov/ccd): The U.S. Department of Education's National Center for Education Statistics (nces.ed.gov) is your best source for local-level educational data, through its CCD program. Information on schools and school districts can be put into custom tables and downloaded in preformatted reports.

Community Economic Development HotReport: See Census Bureau: Community Economic Development HotReport

5-23 Congressional Budget Office: Economic Projections (www.cbo.gov/budget/budget.cfm): Use this source for current national economic projections on such indicators as GDP, unemployment rates, consumer price index, tax bases, and much more.

Consumer Expenditure Survey: See BLS: Consumer Expenditure Survey

County Business Patterns: See Census Bureau: County Business Patterns

5-24 Economics Departments, Institutes and Research Centers in the World (EDIRC; edirc.repec.org/usa.html): Visit this site for a list of links to economic research institutes and university departments. These organizations often produce economic data and provide leads to local economic experts.

5-25 Economic Development Directory (www.ecodevdirectory. com): Economic development organizations collect and share data about companies, industry, employment and unemployment, and other information related to the economic health of local geographic areas. Through this site, you can link to the websites of local groups.

Economy at a Glance: See BLS: Economy at a Glance

5-26 Federal Reserve Board: The Beige Book (www.federalreserve. gov/FOMC/BeigeBook): The central bank of the U.S., the Federal Reserve Board publishes this resource eight times per year. It summarizes current economic conditions by Federal Reserve District and industry sector and is a great source of commentary about regional business activity.

5-27 Federal Reserve Board: Federal Reserve Districts (www.federal reserve.gov/otherfrb.htm): For regional economic data, visit the websites of individual Federal Reserve districts. At this site, you can quickly link to the websites for the 12 local Federal Reserve Districts.

Federal, State, & Local Governments: See Census Bureau: Federal, State, & Local Governments

Geographic Profile of Employment and Unemployment: See BLS: Geographic Profile of Employment and Unemployment

5-28 Google News (news.google.com): Aggregation sites such as Google News help you find news stories about local economic conditions. Go to the advanced search page to search for articles about or from a particular geographic area.

5-29 Housing and Urban Development USER (www.huduser. org/portal): From the U.S. Department of Housing and Urban Development's Office of Policy Development and Research, this site provides current information on housing needs and market conditions.

5-30 InfoUSA.com (www.infousa.com): Through the free features of this site, you can get counts of business establishments by industry, geographic location, and other variables.

Local Area Unemployment Statistics (LAUS): See BLS: Local Area Unemployment Statistics (LAUS)

Local Employment Dynamics (LED): See Census Bureau: Local Employment Dynamics (LED)

Mass Layoff Statistics: See BLS: Mass Layoff Statistics

5-31 National Association of Regional Councils (www.narc.org): To track down local information, try the Regional Council of Governments for your area. These geographically based partnerships often provide economic data on their websites, and you can find these resources through the National Association of Regional Councils site. Just click the Regional Councils/MPOs link.

5-32 News and Newspapers Online (library.uncg.edu/news): Find articles, opinion pieces, research reports, and other resources about the economy through the local press. This directory will take you to links for newspapers and broadcast news outlets throughout the world.

5-33 Newser (www.newser.com): This site collects and summarizes location-based news, which often contains insights into local economies.

5-34 Nielsen Claritas (www.claritas.com): Through the Claritas MarketPlace (www.claritas.com/MarketPlace/Default.jsp), you can find Claritas' own five-year projections for virtually any geographic location.

5-35 O*Net Online (online.onetcenter.org): Funded by the U.S. Department of Labor's Employment & Training Administration, this site provides occupation-related data. Scroll to the bottom of the occupation descriptions to link to state data for 10-year state and national employment trends by occupation.

Occupational Employment Statistics: See BLS: Occupational Employment Statistics

5-36 Radio-Locator (www.radio-locator.com): For local news sources for economic information, don't forget to try radio news outlets. This directory will help you find webpages of and audio streams from private and public radio stations.

5-37 Regional Economic Conditions (www2.fdic.gov/recon): An independent agency of the U.S. government, the Federal Deposit Insurance Corp. offers economic information by geography through this site. Topics include industry activity, employment and income, and real estate activity, and data is presented in a way that makes trends easy to identify.

5-38 Social Security Administration: Geographic Data (www.socialsecurity.gov/policy > Program Statistics and Data Files > By Subject > Geographic Information): Try this resource for state and local statistical reports on topics such as who receives Social Security benefits, earnings and employment data for workers covered by Social Security, and amount of payments, by congressional districts.

5-39 State and Local Government on the Net (www.statelocalgov. net): This directory provides links to both state and local government sites.

5-40 Topix (www.topix.com): Visit this site for location-based news, which often includes articles, opinions, and other information covering local economies.

USA Counties: See Census Bureau: USA Counties

5-41 Yahoo! News (news.yahoo.com): From the main page, follow the Local link for articles organized by geographic location. Look for sources of information about a region's economic health.

5-42 YourEconomy.org (www.youreconomy.org): This excellent resource provides information about business establishments in the U.S., tracked across geographic location, industry, and time. It includes economic information that many other sources don't, such as data on nonemployer firms and startups.

5-43 zapdata (www.zapdata.com): Use this source for information about public and private companies. You can get company counts and market summaries by geographic location, industry, and other variables.

Chapter 6: Local Companies

6-01 American City Business Journals (www.bizjournals.com): These weekly newspapers, published in 40 cities, cover local business news, including hard-to-find information about private companies. Find city of choice and search the site for articles and leads to additional sources.

6-02 AnyWho Yellow Pages (www.anywho.com/yp): Use this online directory to search for businesses by name, location, or distance or browse by state and city.

6-03 ASAE Gateway to Associations Directory (www.asaecenter. org/Community/Directories/associationsearch.cfm): Local organizations are a great resource when you need to fill in the blanks about local companies. Search this site to find organizations by topic and geographic location or reach.

6-04 Bing Maps (www.bing.com/maps): Use this resource to identify companies in a geographic region, read customer reviews, and learn more about a company's physical location.

6-05 Boardreader (www.boardreader.com): This specialized search site helps you search discussions by using company names as keywords.

6-06 BoardTracker (www.boardtracker.com): Search this site, using company names as keywords, for what people are talking about in online discussion forums. This is a useful source for customer opinions and reviews.

6-07 Chamber of Commerce Directory (www.chamberofcommerce. com/chambers): Local chambers of commerce are excellent sources of information about companies located in their geographic region. Follow the links in this directory and search these sites for member directories and the names of key people to call with your questions.

6-08 Copernic Tracker (www.copernic.com): When you're monitoring a company's activities, it's helpful to keep track of any changes to its website. This product is one of several that do this well.

6-09 DexKnows (www.dexknows.com): Find basic company contact information and customer reviews and view a map of the physical location in this online directory.

6-10 Economic Development Directory (www.ecodevdirectory. com): Government and nongovernment economic development organizations often provide useful information about local companies. This resource helps you quickly find and link to the sites of organizations within a particular region.

6-11 Electronic Data Gathering, Analysis, and Retrieval (EDGAR; www.sec.gov/edgar.shtml): Public companies file required forms through the EDGAR system, which can be searched through this site. The site does not offer a way to search by a company's geographic location.

6-12 Facebook (www.facebook.com): This social networking site works best when you need to find information about or make contacts in a known company. Start from your Facebook homepage (free registration required) and enter a company name into the search box.

6-13 Google Blogs Search (blogsearch.google.com): Find what people are saying about companies through blog postings and comments by using companies' names as keywords.

6-14 Google Directory (directory.google.com): Identify and link to the websites of local news outlets through the Regional section of this directory. At these sites, look for articles, interviews, and opinion pieces about local companies.

6-15 Google Maps (maps.google.com): This is a handy resource for identifying companies in a geographic region, reading customer reviews, and—through Street View—viewing physical locations. Also, look for company Place Pages under the More Info link.

6-16 Google News (news.google.com): Through Google's advanced search, you can find news stories from or about a particular geographic location. Look for local news about area companies.

6-17 GuideStar (www2.guidestar.org): Local organizations' websites are an excellent place to look for information about companies based in their geographic region or to learn about local nonprofits. Search GuideStar by topic or geography.

6-18 HelloMetro (www.hellometro.com): This site offers locally
focused articles, reviews, and online discussions. Visit this and
other hyperlocal sites for information about local businesses.

6-19 InfoUSA.com (www.infousa.com): Use the free features on
this site to identify, for example, the number of companies in a
specific industry that have headquarters or offices in a particular
geographic area. This source helps you drill down to the mail-
carrier–route level.

6-20 Internet Archive (www.archive.org): When exploring a company website, take a look at past versions of the site through
Internet Archive, a collection of archived versions of websites
dating back to 1996.

6-21 Kellysearch (www.kellysearch.com): Through this site, you
can look for business-to-business suppliers, leads, and other contacts. Head to the advanced search page, where you can search by
company name, industry, keyword, or city or town.

6-22 LinkedIn (www.linkedin.com): Run a company search directly
from your homepage and filter the results by location and other
variables. To include location in your initial search, go to the
company search page (www.linkedin.com/companies).

6-23 Morningstar Document Research (documentresearch.morning
star.com): This fee-based product helps you search SEC filings
by geography. Look for companies headquartered or doing business in a particular geographic area, and learn more about them
through their filings.

6-24 NewsLink (www.newslink.org): Through this site, you can get
to the websites of local news outlets, which often provide in-
depth coverage of local companies.

6-25 Newspapers.com (www.newspapers.com): As the name
implies, this resource covers just newspapers. The advanced
search page for U.S. newspapers allows you to search by title,
state, city, and frequency.

6-26 Omgili (www.omgili.com): Omgili enables you to search online discussion forums to see what people are saying about local companies and their products or to find people within companies. Through the advanced search page, you can limit your search to keywords that appear in just the discussion title, topic, replies, forum name, and other options, so try using geographic or company names as keywords.

6-27 Outside.in (www.outside.in): Use Outside.in to find hyperlocal articles, online forums, blogs, and reviews. At this site, search by location first. You can then search by business name or other topic.

6-28 Placeblogger (www.placeblogger.com): Visit this site to find hyperlocal blogs that contain information about local companies and their products.

6-29 Superpages.com (www.superpages.com): This online directory is useful for finding contact information about specific companies or identifying companies within a particular geographic area. Use the advanced search feature to search by distance, address, phone number, city, state, ZIP code, or other geographic unit.

6-30 ThomasNet (www.thomasnet.com): This resource offers basic information about manufacturers, distributors, service companies, and manufacturers' representatives. ThomasNet is very useful for locating vendors or finding out how many and what kind of industrial companies operate in a particular place.

6-31 Tourism Offices Worldwide Directory (www.towd.com): Try the official offices of tourism boards and agencies for information about top employers or largest companies in a region. This site includes links to U.S. and non-U.S. groups.

6-32 TweepSearch (tweepsearch.com): This specialized tool helps you search just Twitter profiles to find people connected to a particular company.

6-33 Tweepz (tweepz.com): Try this site to search Twitter profiles (not tweets).

6-34 Twitter (twitter.com): Twitter's 140-character updates often provide insights into the latest company developments and what people have to say about those developments. To search by geography, go to the advanced search page at search.twitter.com.

6-35 WebSite-Watcher (www.aignes.com): This product helps you track any changes to a company website, helping you keep up with the latest developments.

6-36 Yahoo! Directory (dir.yahoo.com): To find the websites of local news outlets, go to the Regional section, and browse by geographic area. These sites often contain news articles, opinion, pieces, blogs, and other sources of information about local companies.

6-37 Yahoo! Maps (maps.yahoo.com): Using this resource, first find a location, using geographic names. Then enter a business category, and you can find and map businesses within a particular geographic area.

6-38 Yahoo! News (news.yahoo.com): Search for local news by using geographic and company names as keywords. Find information about local businesses, including strategy, management changes, product announcements, and more.

6-39 Yelp (www.yelp.com): Select a location, and Yelp creates a page with links to businesses in the area. At this page, you can search further by keyword or browse the list of categories to find customer reviews and maps.

6-40 zapdata (www.zapdata.com): The free features of this site help you determine the number of companies located within a specified geographic area. You can limit your searching by industry, company size, and other variables.

6-41 ZoomInfo (www.zoominfo.com): From the homepage of this people and company directory, click the Company tab and follow the link for advanced search. It offers a geography search feature by country, state, metro region, or ZIP code.

Chapter 7: Looking for Locals

7-01 411 Locate (www.411Locate.com): This online directory is used to find basic contact information for people, including address, phone number, and email.

7-02 ABYZ News Links (www.abyznewslinks.com): This directory is mostly composed of newspaper websites from around the world, but you'll also find some broadcast stations, magazines, and press agencies.

7-03 American City Business Journals (www.bizjournals.com): With weekly newspapers in 40 cities, this is an excellent source for business-related articles about people living in or well-known in a particular geographic area.

7-04 ASAE Gateway to Associations Directory (www.asaecenter. org/Community/Directories/associationsearch.cfm): Tap into the expertise of the people behind local organizations, or use resources from organizations for finding information about local residents. Search this site by topic or geographic area.

7-05 Best of the Web Blog Directory (blogs.botw.org): This directory of location-related blogs from all over the world lets you search by place-name to identify and learn about local experts.

7-06 ChirpCity (chirpcity.com): Use this site to find location-based Twitter updates, which are a great way to find out who's tweeting about what.

7-07 DexKnows (www.dexknows.com): Use this phone-style directory to find basic contact information and to make sure you are researching the correct person.

7-08 Facebook (www.facebook.com): Use this site for connecting with people or identifying leads to people-related information. To find people by location, enter a name or other keyword in the basic search box on your profile page and narrow results by location.

7-09 Globe of Blogs (www.globeofblogs.com): Use this directory to find blogs by geographic location.

7-10 Google Blogs Search (blogsearch.google.com): Identify experts by checking who is blogging and about whom they're writing. Enter people or geographic names as keywords in your search.

7-11 Google Directory (directory.google.com): Turn to regionally focused magazines and news sources to identify local experts and learn more about local people. In the Regional section of this directory, follow the link for News and Media, and you'll find local publications.

7-12 Google Maps (maps.google.com): Use this resource to identify universities in or near a particular geographic area. Click through to the websites of these organizations to find local experts.

7-13 Google News (news.google.com): This resource offers advanced searching by location. Find articles written by or about local experts, or learn more about local celebrities.

7-14 GuideStar (www2.guidestar.org): Tap into the expertise of the people behind local organizations, or use resources from organizations for finding information about local people. The financial filings contained in GuideStar generally provide information about the people within these organizations.

7-15 InOtherNews.us (www.inothernews.us): This site organizes U.S.-based news blogs by state and lets you go beyond the mainstream press.

7-16 iSEEK (www.iseek.com): Through this general-purpose search engine, search for a person's name, and filter the results by location through links on the results page.

7-17 LinkedIn (www.linkedin.com): At LinkedIn, you can search for a particular person or for people who match your criteria. In addition to searching profiles, search LinkedIn groups to find like-minded people, or the Questions and Answers section for subject experts.

7-18 Nearby Tweets (www.nearbytweets.com): This site makes it easy to search Twitter updates by location, which will help you identify and follow local experts.

7-19 NewsVoyager (www.newsvoyager.com): This resource will take you to the websites of daily, weekly, and college newspapers, good sources for coverage of local celebrities and hometown heroes.

7-20 OneRiot (www.oneriot.com): This resource searches social networking sites for current postings by or about people. Enter people or place-names as keywords.

7-21 Peterson's (www.petersons.com): This site is a great tool for quickly identifying all the colleges and universities in or near a particular geographic area. Go to the websites of these institutions to look for and learn more about professors and other experts.

7-22 Pipl (pipl.com): Through Pipl, you can find information about people that has been scraped from social networking sites and other web resources. Always verify the information you find from Pipl, as it has not been vetted by humans.

7-23 Placeblogger (www.placeblogger.com): This directory of location-related blogs from all over the world helps you search by place-name.

7-24 Radio-Locator (www.radio-locator.com): Through this site, you can get to the websites of public and private radio stations, which are great places to look for journalists and other local experts.

7-25 Superpages.com (www.superpages.com): Directory-style sites such as Superpages.com are a good starting place for people-related research. Find and verify basic contact information, searching by first and last names, location, or phone number.

7-26 Technorati (technorati.com): This blog search engine lets you use people and geographic names as keywords and limit your searches to the more-authoritative sites.

7-27 Topix (www.topix.com): Topix gathers and organizes the local news sources by location.

7-28 TV Station Web Page Directory (www.tvwebdirectory. com): This resource provides links to television stations throughout the world, to help you find experts and follow local news.

7-29 Twitter (twitter.com): Head to Twitter's search page (search.twitter.com) and click Advanced Search, where you can find tweets from, to, or about a named person or near a specified geographic area.

7-30 U.S. Universities (www.utexas.edu/world/univ/state): From the University of Texas at Austin, this resource provides links to university websites, organized by name or state. The university sites will lead you to sources of information about local experts.

7-31 Whozat (whozat.com): Search this site to find information about people, including web mentions, social and professional networking sites, images, videos, and Wikipedia (www.wiki pedia.org) references.

7-32 Wink (wink.com): Wink is especially useful for exploring people's social-networking connections. It provides several options for limiting your search using location/distance, interests, schools, groups, career, and tags (descriptive keywords).

7-33 Yahoo! Directory (dir.yahoo.com): Use this resource to identify magazines by location. In the news section, follow the link for magazines, and you'll see a heading for regional publications. These sources often contain in-depth articles about people residing or working within a specific geographic area.

7-34 Yahoo! People (people.yahoo.com): This directory helps you find and verify contact information for people (including email), and it can be searched by name, phone number, or location.

7-35 yoName (www.yoname.com): A people-search engine, this site alerts the person if you search for them by email address, although they won't know who is doing the search.

7-36 ZoomInfo (www.zoominfo.com): This site gathers people-related information from various websites. Make sure you verify what you find, since the information on this site is not verified by people and can be prone to errors.

Chapter 8: Local Issues

8-01 ASAE Gateway to Associations Directory (www.asaecenter. org/Community/Directories/associationsearch.cfm): Visit the websites of local organizations to find information about local issues. Use this resource to find relevant groups by topic or geography.

8-02 Association of State and Territorial Health Officials (www.astho.org): For information about local health issues, visit this site. Here you will find state statistics plus a directory of links to the websites of state health departments, which often provide local-level data.

8-03 BEA (Bureau of Economic Analysis; www.bea.gov): To get an idea of a local area's employment and economic issues, go to the BEA website and click the Regional tab. This page includes several data sets for comparing local-level employment, income, and gross domestic product statistics.

8-04 Common Core of Data (nces.ed.gov/ccd): At this site, you can find information about public schools and districts in the U.S. The data reporting features make it easy to compare results for several geographic locations over time.

8-05 Community Health Status Indicators (www.community health.hhs.gov): These county profiles include data on leading causes of death, relative health importance, vulnerable populations, preventive services, and other indicators. Each profile includes comparisons to peer counties.

8-06 Cyburbia Forums (www.cyburbia.org/forums): This resource, geared toward the urban-planning community, includes online discussion forums covering topics such as urban planning, economic development, sustainability, zoning, and budgeting.

8-07 EveryBlock (www.everyblock.com): Visit EveryBlock for neighborhood-level news and discussions for selected U.S. cities. This site is particularly good at offering insights into life in local communities.

8-08 Federal, State, & Local Governments (www.census.gov/ govs): From the Census Bureau, this site provides information about the financial health of local governments. It includes statistics on government employment and payroll, finances, taxes, libraries, and more.

8-09 Google News (news.google.com): To quickly locate local-level news on any topic, head to this site's advanced search page and search for articles from or about a specific geographic location.

8-10 Google News Archive (news.google.com/archivesearch): At this site, you will find news published more than 30 days in the past. The timeline feature is useful for getting historical overviews of local issues.

8-11 GuideStar (www2.guidestar.org): Use this search tool to find local nonprofit organizations. The people in these groups can often provide insights into local issues and topics of interest.

8-12 HelloMetro (www.hellometro.com): Use this hyperlocal site to find city guides, organized by state, with news, articles, events, and even local tweets.

8-13 InOtherNews.us (www.inothernews.us): Search this collection of U.S.-based news blogs, organized by state, for issues-related news from nonmainstream sources.

8-14 League of Women Voters (www.lwv.org): This organization is an excellent source for unbiased information about local political issues. Visit the league's website to find local chapters.

8-15 Libweb Library Directory (lists.webjunction.org/libweb): Many library websites include sections with resources covering local issues. This directory includes links to the websites of libraries of all types in 146 countries, organized by location.

8-16 LocalSchoolDirectory.com (www.localschooldirectory.com): This specialty site offers detailed information about local schools and districts, including funding, class size, student achievement, and more.

8-17 MSNBC.com (www.msnbc.msn.com): From this page, follow the link for Local News and click on any state to view a list of cities with MSNBC affiliates. For each of the affiliates, you can view news about local issues from the affiliates' cities and nearby cities.

8-18 National Association of Counties (www.naco.org): Obtain county-level information from this organization on a wide range of issues. At this site, you will find statistics, survey results, and publications on a variety of topics, including the environment, energy, land use, public safety, transportation, and more.

8-19 News and Newspapers Online (library.uncg.edu/news): This site offers a compilation of links to the websites of newspapers and broadcast news outlets throughout the world. Search these websites for articles with information about the issues and hot topics in a particular geographic location, or look for leads to sources.

8-20 Omgili (www.omgili.com): Use this search tool to monitor online discussion groups for information about local, issues-related topics. Use keywords and geographic names in your searching.

8-21 OneRiot (www.oneriot.com): This specialized site gathers what people are saying on Twitter, Facebook, and other social sites into one convenient place. There's no advanced searching, so try using location names in your search.

8-22 Outside.in (www.outside.in): Enter an address, a neighborhood, or a city to get to local news and information about local issues, culled from news sites, blogs, and online discussions.

8-23 Placeblogger (www.placeblogger.com): Placeblogger will help you find hyperlocal blogs all over the world in order to gain an insider's view of the politics, lifestyle, and social issues of cities, towns, and neighborhoods.

8-24 Sierra Club (www.sierraclub.org): Visit this resource to get to the websites of local chapters of this national organization. You can look for online resources covering local environmental issues and identify people to call for research help.

8-25 Silobreaker (www.silobreaker.com): Enter a city or state and search for news from or about that location. The network page helps you see connections to people, topics, or organizations related to your search.

8-26 Sperling's Best Places (www.bestplaces.net): This well-known site is an excellent resource for learning about a local area's quality of life and other issues. Search for a U.S. city, town, or ZIP code to find data on demographics, cost of living, housing, school spending, unemployment, religion, and more.

8-27 State and Local Government on the Net (www.statelocal gov.net): This directory of links to specific state, regional, county, city, and town governing bodies will help you find insights into a geographic region's governing processes and jurisdictions.

8-28 Stateline.org (www.stateline.org): Visit this site for state-oriented news stories, links to elected officials, state legislative summaries, and state-by-state summaries of various political issues, many of which originate at the local level.

8-29 Trulia (www.trulia.com): This real-estate site includes an interesting collection of statistics, housing-market trends, and school and community information.

8-30 Twitter (twitter.com): See what local issues people are currently talking about. For location-based searching, use Twitter's advanced search feature (search.twitter.com).

8-31 Uniform Crime Reports (www.fbi.gov/ucr/ucr.htm): From the Federal Bureau of Investigation, this site provides crime statistics for regions, states, counties, cities, metropolitan statistical areas, and even individual universities and colleges (organized by state).

8-32 USA.gov: Local Governments: (www.usa.gov/Agencies/ Local.shtml): This resource will help you find state, regional, and local governments on the web, which often have statistics, regulatory updates, infrastructure developments, and other information about local issues.

8-33 Yahoo! News (news.yahoo.com): Follow the Local link, select any U.S. city or ZIP code, and view top news headlines and current events for the region. This provides a nice snapshot of current local issues.

Chapter 9: Paying at the Pump

9-01 ACCRA Cost of Living Index (www.coli.org): Use this source for city-by-city cost-of-living comparisons. This is helpful for people or companies relocating to a new area and for when you're trying to understand target geographic markets.

9-02 Acxiom (www.acxiom.com): Go to this resource for consumer lists, compiled through public records, census data, surveys, catalog companies, and other list providers. Customize lists by geography, demographics, and psychographics.

9-03 BizMiner (www.bizminer.com): Well known for its industry analysis reports, this resource currently offers three geography-based products for identifying local industry trends: Local Market Research Reports, Competitive Market Analyzer, and Regional Business Profiles.

9-04 Claritas MarketPlace (www.claritas.com/MarketPlace/Default. jsp): Through its Claritas MarketPlace site, Nielsen Claritas sells several low-cost reports and maps, customized by geography. These products are an excellent source for demographics, including five-year projections, for small geographic units.

Cost of Living Index: See ACCRA Cost of Living Index

9-05 Dialog (www.dialog.com): This database product used by professional researchers compiles information from many reliable sources, provides advanced searching for drilling to the local level, and offers specialized local content.

9-06 Dun & Bradstreet (www.dnb.com): Dun & Bradstreet provides business lists of public and private companies, compiled through public records and directories. Data can be customized by geography, job title, company size, and industry.

9-07 Equifax (www.equifax.com): Through this resource, you can purchase business lists, customized by geography, job title, revenues, number of employees, and industry.

9-08 Esri (www.esri.com): This company offers geographic information system software and services and location-based data, including demographics, consumer spending, market potential, geographic maps and aerial imagery, and traffic counts.

9-09 Experian (www.experian.com): One of the major sources of business leads and direct mailing lists, this resource will create customized lists by geography and other variables.

9-10 Factiva (www.factiva.com): This resource, used by many professional researchers, includes specialized tools and content that help you quickly find articles, reports, and other sources of local information.

9-11 Hoover's (www.hoovers.com): This subscription-based product provides business lists with public and private companies. Lists can be created according to geographic location, company size, and other variables.

9-12 InfoUSA.com (www.infousa.com): One of several mailing list and list service providers, this resource helps identify and count buyers and competitors, based on geography. You can get business or name counts for free. For a fee, you have the ability to download lists, with unlimited use for one year.

9-13 LexisNexis (www.lexisnexis.com): A subscription-based resource geared toward professional researchers, this product includes specialized content and features for finding local-level information.

9-14 Moody's Analytics Research Store (www.economy.com/
store): At this site, you can purchase individual Moody's reports
and tables that focus on smaller geographic units. The easiest
way to find products with local-level information is through the
U.S. Metro Areas link.

9-15 Morningstar Document Research (documentresearch.morning
star.com): This is a powerful tool for searching SEC filings for information about companies, products, and markets. Special geographic-
search features help you quickly drill to the local level.

9-16 NewsLibrary.com (nl.newsbank.com): A database of articles
from thousands of U.S. newspapers, this resource is searchable
by region, state, or a specific newspaper. Purchase individual articles or a monthly subscription, which allows you to view, print,
and save up to 25 articles per month.

9-17 NextMark, www.nextmark.com: This source, used by many
professional list brokers, is for buying and selling business lists.

Nielsen Claritas: See Claritas MarketPlace

9-18 PolicyMap (www.policymap.com): A provider of maps and
mapping services, PolicyMap offers a vast collection of data that
can be saved easily in nicely formatted reports, maps, and tables.
It's an excellent source of information about the health of a local
economy and a good choice when you need to compare data
across geographic locations or view trends over time.

9-19 Standard Rate Data Service (www.srds.com): Like NextMark,
this site is generally used by professional list brokers to purchase
reliable, customized business mailing lists.

How Do I ...?: Short Guides to Local Business Research

This appendix includes short guides to using the web for typical local business and market research. It contains research scenarios and lists resources that will help you handle each situation. The numbers listed in parentheses indicate where in Appendix A you will find more information about using each site.

Make sure to periodically check www.ResearchOnMain Street.com for updates to these and all resources mentioned in this book.

I need data on businesses, including nonemployer firms.
YourEconomy.org (5-42), www.youreconomy.org
Census Bureau: Nonemployer Statistics (2-26), www.census.gov/
    econ/nonemployer

*I'm looking for an easy way to identify college newspapers within
    a particular geographic region.*

ABYZ News Links (2-01), www.abyznewslinks.com
Google Directory (7-11), directory.google.com
NewsVoyager (7-19), www.newsvoyager.com

I want to track down historical census data.
Census Bureau (2-17), www.census.gov
Historical Census Browser (4-14), mapserver.lib.virginia.edu
Social Explorer (4-19), www.socialexplorer.com

I need to learn more about recent management changes within a
   particular company.
American City Business Journals (6-01), www.bizjournals.com
EDGAR (6-11), www.sec.gov/edgar.shtml
Morningstar Document Research (9-15), documentresearch.
   morningstar.com

I need information about the veteran population.
Census Bureau: American Community Survey (2-19),
   factfinder.census.gov
National Center for Veterans Analysis and Statistics (4-17),
   www.va.gov/vetdata

I need info on a local source outside the U.S.
Feedmap (2-41), www.feedmap.net
Tourism Offices Worldwide Directory (6-31), www.towd.com
ABYZ News Links (7-02), www.abyznewslinks.com
Best of the Web Blog Directory (7-05), blogs.botw.org
Placeblogger (7-23), www.placeblogger.com

I need population projections for several ZIP codes.
Claritas MarketPlace (9-04), www.claritas.com/MarketPlace/
   Default.jsp

I'm looking for information about older Americans.

Census Bureau: American Community Survey (2-19), factfinder.
census.gov

Social Security Administration: Geographic Data (5-38),
www.socialsecurity.gov/policy > Program Statistics and Data
Files > By Subject > Geographic Information

*I'm trying to find information about the quality of the local school
system.*

School District Demographics System (4-18), nces.ed.gov/
surveys/sdds

Common Core of Data (5-22), www.nces.ed.gov/ccd

LocalSchoolDirectory.com (8-16), www.localschooldirectory.com

Sperling's Best Places (8-26), www.bestplaces.net

I'd like some help finding local vendors.

DexKnows (6-09), www.dexknows.com

Kellysearch (6-21), www.kellysearch.com

ThomasNet (6-30), www.thomasnet.com

I'd like to find customer reviews of my competitors' businesses.

DexKnows (6-09), www.dexknows.com

Outside.in (6-27), www.outside.in

Yelp (6-39), www.yelp.com

I need information about my competitors' strategies.

American City Business Journals (6-01), www.bizjournals.com

EDGAR (6-11), www.sec.gov/edgar.shtml

WebSite-Watcher (6-35), www.aignes.com

Yahoo! News (6-38), news.yahoo.com

*I need statistics on the number of children living in poverty in
several cities.*

Census Bureau: American Community Survey (2-19),
  factfinder.census.gov
Census Bureau: Small Area Income and Poverty Estimates (2-28),
  www.census.gov/did/www/saipe

I'm looking for free economic projections.
Congressional Budget Office: Economic Projections (5-23),
  www.cbo.gov/budget/budget.cfm
O*Net Online (5-35), online.onetcenter.org

I need information about crime in a particular geographic area.
Fwix (2-43), fwix.com
Census Bureau: USA Counties (4-09),
  censtats.census.gov/usa/usa.shtml
Uniform Crime Reports (8-31), www.fbi.gov/ucr/ucr.htm

I'm trying to find historical labor force data for local areas.
Census Bureau: County Business Patterns (through CenStats)
  (2-24), censtats.census.gov
BLS: Economy at a Glance (5-07), www.bls.gov/eag
BLS: Geographic Profile of Employment and Unemployment
  (5-09), www.bls.gov/gps

I need statistics on personal income for local areas.
BEA: Local Area Personal Income and Employment (2-06),
  www.bea.gov/regional
BEA Regional Fact Sheets (2-08), www.bea.gov/regional
BEA: Bureau of Economic Analysis (5-04), www.bea.gov
Regional Economic Conditions (5-37), www2.fdic.gov/recon

I'm trying to search Twitter updates by location.
Localtweeps (2-56), www.localtweeps.com
Nearby Tweets (2-59), www.nearbytweets.com

Twitter (6-34), twitter.com
TwellowHood (2-78), www.twellow.com/twellowhood

I want some data related to commute times to work.
Census Bureau: American Community Survey (2-19),
    factfinder.census.gov
Sperling's Best Places (8-26), www.bestplaces.net

*I want to find employment data that's broken down by geography
    and occupation.*
BLS: Occupational Employment Statistics (5-12), www.bls.gov/
    OES
PolicyMap (9-18), www.policymap.com

*I'm looking for information to help me compare the cost of living
    in several cities.*
Bureau of Labor Statistics (2-10), www.bls.gov
Sperling's Best Places (8-26), www.bestplaces.net
ACCRA Cost of Living Index (9-01), www.coli.org

*I'd like to be able to find people in a certain geographic area with
    common areas of interest.*
Facebook (7-08), www.facebook.com
LinkedIn (7-17), www.linkedin.com
Wink (7-32), wink.com

I'm looking for statistics on economic growth.
Census Bureau: Local Employment Dynamics (5-18),
    lehd.did.census.gov/led/led/led.html
YourEconomy.org (5-42), www.youreconomy.org

I need to find data covering farming and ranching operations.
Census of Agriculture (5-20), www.agcensus.usda.gov

I'm looking for information about local politics.
League of Women Voters (8-14), www.lwv.org
Placeblogger (8-23), www.placeblogger.com
State and Local Government on the Net (8-27), www.statelocal
    gov.net
Stateline.org (8-28), www.stateline.org

I need to identify companies with headquarters in a particular city.
Chamber of Commerce Directory (6-07), www.chamberof
    commerce.com/chambers
EDGAR (6-11), www.sec.gov/edgar.shtml
InfoUSA.com (9-12), www.infousa.com

I'd like to search some alternative news sources.
ABYZ News Links (7-02), www.abyznewslinks.com
InOtherNews.us (7-15), www.inothernews.us
EveryBlock (8-07), www.everyblock.com

I need information about metro-area business vacancies.
Economic Development Directory (5-25),
    www.ecodevdirectory.com
HUD USER (5-29), www.huduser.org/portal
ASAE Gateway to Associations Directory (7-04), www.asae
    center.org/Community/Directories/associationsearch.cfm

I need a source for finding email addresses.
411 Locate (7-01), www.411Locate.com
Pipl (7-22), pipl.com
ZoomInfo (7-36), www.zoominfo.com

*I'd like to understand the current state of the housing market in
    several metropolitan areas.*

Economic Development Directory (5-25),
   www.ecodevdirectory.com
HUD USER (5-29), www.huduser.org/portal
Trulia (8-29), www.trulia.com

I need to find information about private companies.
American City Business Journals (6-01), www.bizjournals.com
Dun & Bradstreet (9-06), www.dnb.com
Hoover's (9-11), www.hoovers.com

I'd like to check for local news in sources other than newspapers.
Radio-Locator (2-67), www.radio-locator.com
TV Station Web Page Directory (7-28), www.tvwebdirectory.com
MSNBC.com (8-17), www.msnbc.msn.com

I need to learn about my constituents.
Census Bureau: American Community Survey (4-02),
   factfinder.census.gov
Claritas MarketPlace (4-10), www.claritas.com/MarketPlace/
   Default.jsp
National Center for Veterans Analysis and Statistics (4-17),
   www.va.gov/vetdata
EveryBlock (8-07), www.everyblock.com

I'd like to verify an expert's credentials.
LinkedIn (2-54), www.linkedin.com
BNET (3-03), www.bnet.com
U.S. Universities (7-30), www.utexas.edu/world/univ/state
ZoomInfo (7-36), www.zoominfo.com

*I'm looking for data on the strength of the housing market within
   the metropolitan area.*

Census Bureau: Building Permits (5-14), censtats.census.gov/
    bldg/bldginfo.shtml
HUD USER (5-29), www.huduser.org/portal
Trulia (8-29), www.trulia.com

*I need to identify nonprofit organizations within a particular geo-
    graphic area.*
ASAE Gateway to Associations Directory (7-04), www.asae
    center.org/Community/Directories/associationsearch.cfm
GuideStar (8-11), www2.guidestar.org

*I'd like some information about the libraries within a particular
    geographic region.*
Census Bureau: Federal, State, & Local Governments (5-17),
    www.census.gov/govs
Common Core of Data (5-22), nces.ed.gov/ccd
Libweb Library Directory (8-15), lists.webjunction.org/libweb

*I need statistics covering business startups, broken down to the
    local level.*
YourEconomy.org (2-86), www.youreconomy.org
BizMiner (9-03), www.bizminer.com

*I need to contact people who have recently worked for a particular
    company.*
LinkedIn (7-17), www.linkedin.com
Pipl (7-22), pipl.com

I'm looking for local-level economic projections.
GovEngine.com (4-12), www.govengine.com
Association for University Business and Economic Research
    (5-03), www.auber.org

EDIRC: Economics Departments, Institutes and Research Centers in the World (5-24), edirc.repec.org/usa.html

Moody's Analytics Research Store (9-14), www.economy.com/store

I need to track monthly trends in local employment.

BLS: Economy at a Glance (5-07), www.bls.gov/eag

BLS: Local Area Unemployment Statistics (5-10), www.bls.gov/lau

I'd like to compare employment figures for several geographic areas.

BLS: Occupational Employment Statistics (5-12), www.bls.gov/OES

Bureau of Economic Analysis (8-03), www.bea.gov

I need a source that will help me identify economic trends over time.

Census Bureau: Local Employment Dynamics Program (5-18), lehd.did.census.gov/led/led/led.html

Regional Economic Conditions (5-37), www2.fdic.gov/recon

PolicyMap (9-18), www.policymap.com

I want to identify geographic areas in which there have been recent mass layoffs.

BLS: Mass Layoff Statistics (5-11), www.bls.gov/data

Google News (5-28), news.google.com

I need mapped industry data.

BEA: Gross Domestic Product (GDP) by State and Metropolitan Area (2-05), www.bea.gov/regional

Claritas MarketPlace (9-04), www.claritas.com/MarketPlace/Default.jsp

I need to identify the largest employers in a particular geographic region.

Economic Development Directory (5-25),
    www.ecodevdirectory.com

Chamber of Commerce Directory (6-07), www.chamberof
    commerce.com/chambers

InfoUSA.com (9-12), www.infousa.com

I'd like to have current news for a particular geographic location compiled in one webpage.

Yahoo! News (5-41), news.yahoo.com

Topix (7-27), www.topix.com

I need to monitor what people are saying in online discussion groups.

Boardreader (6-05), www.boardreader.com

Omgili (6-26), www.omgili.com

Outside.in (6-27), www.outside.in

I'm researching metropolitan-area consumer spending trends.

BLS: Consumer Expenditure Survey (5-06), www.bls.gov/cex

Esri (9-08), www.esri.com

About the Author

Marcy Phelps is the president of Phelps Research, which provides professional research and research training services that help clients find and use strategic business information. She founded the company in 2000 after obtaining a master's degree in library and information services from the University of Denver. She is a past president of the Association of Independent Information Professionals (www.aiip.org).

Marcy is a contributing editor for FUMSI (www.fumsi.com), a publication for people who find, use, manage, and share information. She frequently writes and speaks on a variety of topics, from business and networking skills to finding and evaluating information on the web. She also blogs about turning information into insights at www.MarcyPhelps.com.

A first-degree black belt in tae kwon do, Marcy lives in Lakewood, Colorado, with her husband and their two dogs.

241

INDEX

More Great Books from Information Today, Inc.

Building & Running a Successful Research Business, 2nd Edition
A Guide for the Independent Information Professional

By Mary Ellen Bates
Foreword by Amelia Kassel

This is the handbook every aspiring independent information professional needs in order to launch, manage, and build a research business. Author Mary Ellen Bates covers everything from "Is this right for you?" to closing the sale, managing clients, promoting your business on the web, and tapping into powerful information sources beyond the web. The second edition features a wealth of new material, including new chapters on how to position yourself, marketing via social media, creating an effective web presence, strategic planning for your next five years, and writing a marketing plan that works.

528 pp/softbound/ISBN 978-0-910965-85-9 $34.95

Dancing With Digital Natives
Staying in Step With the Generation That's Transforming the Way Business Is Done

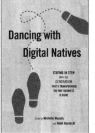

Edited by Michelle Manafy and Heidi Gautschi

Generational differences have always influenced how business is done, but in the case of digital natives—those immersed in digital technology from birth—we are witnessing a tectonic shift. As an always connected, socially networked generation increasingly dominates business and society, organizations can ignore the implications only at the risk of irrelevance. In this fascinating book, Michelle Manafy, Heidi Gautschi, and a stellar assemblage of experts from business and academia provide vital insights into the characteristics of this transformative generation. Here is an in-depth look at how digital natives work, shop, play and learn, along with practical advice geared to help managers, marketers, coworkers, and educators maximize their interactions and create environments where everyone wins.

400 pp/hardbound/ISBN 978-0-910965-87-3 $27.95

The Internet Book of Life
Use the Web to Grow Richer, Smarter, Healthier, and Happier

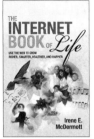

By Irene E. McDermott

No matter what you want to accomplish in life, there are quality, free online resources available to help—if you only had the time to find and evaluate them all! Now, noted author, columnist, reference librarian, and working mom Irene McDermott rides to the rescue with *The Internet Book of Life*—a handy guide to websites, blogs, online tools, and mobile apps. From matters of personal finance to parenting, relationships, health and medicine, careers, travel, hobbies, pets, home improvement, and more, each chapter addresses real-life goals, dilemmas, and solutions. *The Internet Book of Life*—along with its supporting blog—is the lively, indispensable reference that belongs next to every home computer.

304 pp/softbound/ISBN 978-0-910965-89-7 $19.95

The Extreme Searcher's Internet Handbook, 3rd Edition
A Guide for the Serious Searcher

By Randolph Hock

The Extreme Searcher's Internet Handbook is the essential guide for anyone who uses the internet for research—librarians, teachers, students, writers, business professionals, and others who need to search the web proficiently. In this fully updated third edition, Ran Hock covers strategies and tools for all major areas of internet content. Readers with little to moderate searching experience will appreciate Hock's helpful, easy-to-follow advice, while experienced searchers will discover a wealth of new ideas, techniques, and resources.

368 pp/softbound/ISBN 978-0-910965-84-2 $24.95